Hard to elude
is the reach of Death,
Hard to pass beyond.
But they who accord
with the Dhamma well taught,
they will pass beyond.

Dhammapada, *verse 86*

Seeing the Way

Buddhist Reflections on
the Spiritual Life

AMARAVATI PUBLICATIONS

FOR FREE DISTRIBUTION
Publications from Amaravati are for free
distribution. In most cases, this is made possible
through offerings from individuals or groups, given
specifically for the publication of Buddhist teachings.
Further information is available from the address below.

Sabbadānaṁ dhammadānaṁ jināti
'The gift of Dhamma surpasses all other gifts.'

Published by
Amaravati Publications
Amaravati Buddhist Centre
Great Gaddesden
Hemel Hempstead
Hertfordshire HP1 3BZ
England

© Amaravati Publications 1989

ISBN   1 870205 04 9

Printed in Thailand by
Amarin Printing Group Co., Ltd.
Tel. 4242800-1

CONTENTS

DEDICATION

**Yo Dhammam desesi: adhikalyanam,
majjhekalyanam, pariyosanakalyanam.**

*The Buddha has pointed out the way:
beautiful in the beginning, beautiful in the middle,
and beautiful in the end.*

Each morning in Theravada Buddhist monasteries around the world, the above stanza is chanted as part of 'The Homage to the Triple Gem'. It could just as well be said of the teaching example of Meditation Master, The Venerable Ajahn Chah.

Ajahn Chah, or *Luang Por* as his disciples called him, possessed that uniquely beautiful quality of being: a quality visible only to a heart seeking The Way of Truth.

'Beautiful in the beginning', in Ajahn Chah's case, was his commitment to the life of a renunciant monk (*dhutanga bhikkhu*). He cultivated impeccable discipline and displayed consistent, daring effort to confront all situations, especially those from which he was inclined to turn away. He gave himself completely to the training and eventually the Way became clear.

'Beautiful in the middle' was the selfless sharing of his realization with all who came to be near him. Regardless of personal discomfort, he ceaselessly offered his body, speech and mind to assist his disciples, lay and ordained alike, to enter the Way. He said of his own teaching method, that it is the example that counts – not just the words. Those who were able to spend time with him know full well that this is so.

And 'beautiful in the end' remains. It is that radiant confidence of heart in thousands of individuals who now walk the Way; that verified faith which most profoundly expresses *Dhammam Saranam Gacchami* – 'I go for refuge to the Truth of the Way Things Are.' Without having seen an example of the Way in another, such awakening of confidence might not have taken place; hence it is said, 'No gift excels the gift of Dhamma.'

INTRODUCTION

No amount of words can possibly honour a gift as precious as the
Way of Truth itself. Lives lived in harmony with this Ancient
Way, however, may do so.

This book is about a community of people endeavouring to do
justice to the gift they have received. More precisely, it is a
collection of transcribed talks, letters and essays offered by
disciples of Luang Por Chah, who are now living at various
monasteries around the world. These teachings have been
gathered specifically for this publication. It seemed appropriate
that a book published in the West to honour the Venerable Ajahn
Chah's life should reflect the results of his years of teaching. These
are some of the fruits of what he spent his life nurturing.
Although some editing was required so that the oral teachings
might be accessible in the written form, it is hoped that the spirit
of the original presentation has been preserved: that is, the spirit
of the living Truth.

The Buddha said that nobody else can walk the Way for us – but
they can point out the way we should go. The directions given will
be different for each of us, depending on how far we must go and
from where we are starting. There were occasions when people
questioned Ajahn Chah about apparent contradictions in his
advice. He replied that if he was standing at the end of a road and
saw someone coming towards him veering off to the left, he would
tell them to go right. If they were veering to the right he would
tell them to move left. The instructions were different, but the
ultimate direction was the same.

Style and emphasis also vary when the Teaching is presented by
different individuals. This will become obvious as the reader
progresses through this book. The reader may also come across
inconsistencies and contradictions. If this is so, it should be
remembered that such discrepancies are in appearance only. These
words are not presented as the Truth itself but as reflections
offered for consideration.

Many people have benefitted from Ajahn Chah's ability to point out the Way; and many of these same people have participated in offering this book in commemoration of their teacher. One of the deepest forms of gratitude is that which springs forth from a true appreciation for the beauty of the Way; it is with such gratitude that this offering is made. It is the wish of all who have contributed, that the readers may see, understand, and follow the Way about which all these words have been written.

EVAM

A NOTE ON HIERARCHY AND THE ORDER OF PRESENTATION

The Buddha instructed that respect should always be shown to those monks who have been in the Order the longest. This holds true regardless of other qualities any individual may possess. Hence, the sequence of this presentation is determined solely in accordance with seniority in the *bhikkhu-sangha*. These talks are not offered as a progressive teaching. Accordingly, it is recommended that readers feel free to select and read, re-read or omit as they wish.

T. YESHE

VENERABLE AJAHN CHAH

VENERABLE AJAHN CHAH was born on June 17, 1918 in a small village near the town of Ubon Rajathani, North-East Thailand.

After finishing his basic schooling, he spent three years as a novice before returning to lay life to help his parents on the farm. At the age of twenty, however, he decided to resume monastic life, and on April 26, 1939 he received *upasampada* (bhikkhu ordination).

Ajahn Chah's early monastic life followed a traditional pattern, of studying Buddhist teachings and the Pali scriptural language. In his fifth year his father fell seriously ill and died, a blunt reminder of the frailty and precariousness of human life. It caused him to think deeply about life's real purpose, for although he had studied extensively and gained some proficiency in Pali, he seemed no nearer to a personal understanding of the end of suffering. Feelings of disenchantment set in, and finally (in 1946) he abandoned his studies and set off on mendicant pilgrimage.

He walked some 400 km to Central Thailand, sleeping in forests and gathering almsfood in the villages on the way. He took up residence in a monastery where the *vinaya* (monastic discipline) was carefully studied and practised. While there he was told about Venerable Ajahn Mun Buridatto, a most highly respected Meditation Master. Keen to meet such an accomplished teacher, Ajahn Chah set off on foot for the North-East in search of him.

At this time Ajahn Chah was wrestling with a crucial problem. He had studied the teachings on morality, meditation and wisdom, which the texts presented in

minute and refined detail, but he could not see how they could actually be put into practice. Ajahn Mun told him that although the teachings are indeed extensive, at their heart they are very simple. With mindfulness established, if it is seen that everything arises in the heart-mind... right there is the true path of practice. This succinct and direct teaching was a revelation for Ajahn Chah, and transformed his approach to practice. The Way was clear.

For the next seven years Ajahn Chah practised in the style of the austere Forest Tradition, wandering through the countryside in quest of quiet and secluded places for developing meditation. He lived in tiger- and cobra-infested jungles, using reflections on death to penetrate to the true meaning of life. On one occasion he practised in a cremation ground, to challenge and eventually overcome his fear of death. Then, as he sat cold and drenched in a rain storm, he faced the utter desolation and loneliness of a homeless monk.

In 1954, after years of wandering, he was invited back to his home village. He settled close by, in a fever-ridden, haunted forest called 'Pah Pong'. Despite the hardships of malaria, poor shelter and sparse food, disciples gathered around him in increasing numbers. The monastery which is now known as Wat Pah Pong began there, and eventually branch monasteries were also established elsewhere.

In 1967 an American monk came to stay at Wat Pah Pong. The newly ordained Venerable Sumedho had just spent his first *vassa* ('Rains' retreat) practising intensive meditation at a monastery near the Laotian border.

Although his efforts had borne some fruit, Venerable Sumedho realized that he needed a teacher who could train him in all aspects of monastic life. By chance, one of Ajahn Chah's monks – one who happened to speak a little English! – visited the monastery where Venerable Sumedho was staying. Upon hearing about Ajahn Chah, he asked to take leave of his preceptor, and went back to Wat Pah Pong with the monk.

Ajahn Chah willingly accepted the new disciple, but insisted that he receive no special allowances for being a Westerner. He would have to eat the same simple almsfood and practise in the same way as any other monk at Wat Pah Pong.

The training there was quite harsh and forbidding. Ajahn Chah often pushed his monks to their limits, to test their powers of endurance so that they would develop patience and resolution. He sometimes initiated long and seemingly pointless work projects, in order to frustrate their attachment to tranquillity. The emphasis was always on surrender to the way things are, and great stress was placed upon strict observance of the *vinaya.*

In the course of events, other Westerners came through Wat Pah Pong. By the time Venerable Sumedho was a bhikkhu of five *vassas,* and Ajahn Chah considered him competent enough to teach, some of these new monks had also decided to stay on and train there.

In the hot season of 1975, Venerable Sumedho and a handful of Western bhikkhus spent some time living in a forest not far from Wat Pah Pong. The local villagers there asked them to stay on, and Ajahn Chah consented. Thus Wat Pah Nanachat ('International

Forest Monastery') came into being, and Venerable Sumedho became the abbot of the first monastery in Thailand to be run by and for English-speaking monks.

In 1977, Ajahn Chah was invited to visit Britain by the English Sangha Trust, a charity with the aim of establishing a locally-resident Buddhist Sangha. He took Venerable Sumedho and Venerable Khemadhammo along, and seeing the serious interest there, left them in London at the Hampstead Vihara (with two of his other Western disciples who were then visiting Europe).

He returned to Britain in 1979, at which time the monks were leaving London to begin Chithurst Buddhist Monastery in Sussex. He then went on to America and Canada to visit and teach.

After this trip, and again in 1981, Ajahn Chah spent the 'Rains' away from Wat Pah Pong, since his health was failing due to the debilitating effects of diabetes. As his illness worsened, he would use his body as a teaching, a living example of the impermanence of all things. He constantly reminded people to endeavour to find a true refuge within themselves, since he would not be able to teach for very much longer.

Before the end of the 'Rains' of 1981, he was taken to Bangkok for an operation; it, however, did little to improve his condition. Within a few months he stopped talking, and gradually he lost control of his limbs until he was virtually paralysed and bed-ridden. From then on, he was diligently and lovingly nursed and attended by devoted disciples, grateful for the occasion to offer service to the teacher who so patiently and compassionately showed the Way to so many.

A MESSAGE FROM THAILAND

The following message by Venerable Ajahn Chah was sent to his disciples in England whilst he was resident at a branch monastery called 'The Cave of Diamond Light', just prior to the serious decline in his health during the Rainy-Season Retreat (Vassa) of 1981. A photograph taken at the time of recording this message on tape appears on the back cover. 'Wat Pah Pong', referred to near the end of the text, is the name of Ajahn Chah's main monastery.

I HAVE COME UP TO WAT TUM SAENG PET for the 'Rains' Retreat this year – mostly for a change of air as my health has not been so good. With me are a few Western monks: Santa, Pabhakaro, Pamutto, Michael and *Samanen* Guy; also some Thai monks and a small number of lay people who are keen to practice. This is a pleasant and fortunate time for us. At the moment my sickness has subsided, so I feel well enough to record this message for you all.

Because of this ill-health I cannot visit England, so hearing news of you, from some of your supporters who are staying here, has made me very happy and relieved. The thing that pleases me most is that Sumedho is now able to ordain monks; this shows that your efforts to establish Buddhism in England have been quite successful.

It is also pleasing to see the names of the monks and nuns whom I know, who are living with Sumedho at Chithurst: Anando, Viradhammo, Sucitto, Uppanno, Kittisaro, and Amaro. Also Mae Chees Rocana and Candasiri. I hope you are all in good health and living harmoniously together, co-operating and proceeding well in Dhamma practice.

There are supporters, both in England and here in Thailand, who help keep me up to date with your developments. I gather from them that the building work at Chithurst is complete, and that it is now a much more comfortable place to live. I often enquire about this, as I remember my stay of seven days there was quite difficult! (laughter) I hear that the shrine-room and the other

21

main areas are now all finished. With less building work to be carried out, the community will be able to apply itself more fully to formal practice.

I understand also that some of the senior monks have been moved off to start branch monasteries. This is normal practice, but it can lead to a predominance of junior monks at the main monastery; this has been the case in the past at Wat Pah Pong. This can bring difficulties in the teaching and training of monks, so it is very important in these situations that we help one another.

I trust that Sumedho is not allowing these sort of things to burden him! These are small matters, quite normal, they are not a problem at all. Certainly there are responsibilities – but it can also be seen that there are none.

To be the abbot of a monastery can be compared to being a rubbish bin: those who are disturbed by the presence of rubbish make a bin, in the hope that people will put their rubbish in there. In actual fact what happens is that the person who makes the bin ends up being the rubbish collector as well. This is how things are – it's the same at Wat Pah Pong, it was the same at the time of the Buddha. No-one else puts the rubbish into it so we have to do it ourselves, and everything gets chucked into the abbot's bin!

One in such a position must therefore be far-sighted, have depth, and remain unshaken in the midst of all things; they must be consistent – able to persevere. Of all the qualities we develop in our lives, patient endurance is the *most* important.

It is true that the establishment of a suitable dwelling place at Chithurst has been completed – the construction of a building is not difficult, a couple of years and it is done. What has not been completed, though, is the work of upkeep and maintenance – the sweeping, washing and so forth have to go on forever. It is not difficult to build a monastery, but it is difficult to maintain it; likewise, it is not difficult to ordain someone, but to train them fully in the monastic life is hard. This should not be taken as a problem, though, for to do that which is hard is very beneficial –

doing only that which is easy does not have much use. Therefore, in order to nurture and maintain the seed of Buddhism which has been planted at Chithurst, you must now all be prepared to put forth your energies and help.

I hope that what I have said today has conveyed feelings of warmth and support to you. Whenever I meet Thai people who have connections in England, I ask if they have been to visit Chithurst. It seems, from them, that there is a great deal of interest in a branch monastery being there. Also, foreigners who come here will frequently have visited Wat Nanachat and have news of you in England as well. It makes me very happy to see that there is such a close and co-operative relationship between Wat Pah Pong, Wat Nanachat and Wat Chithurst.

That is all I have to say, except that my feelings of loving-kindness are with you all. May you be well and happy, abiding in harmony, co-operation and togetherness. May the blessings of the Buddha, the Dhamma and the Sangha always be firmly established in your hearts – may you be well.

WHAT IS CONTEMPLATION?

The following teaching is taken from a session of questions and answers that took place at Wat Gor Nork monastery during the Vassa of 1979, between Venerable Ajahn Chah and a group of English-speaking disciples. Some rearrangement of the sequence of conversation has been made for ease of understanding.

The knowing that arises is above and beyond the process of thinking. It leads to not being fooled by thinking any more.

QUESTION: *When you teach about the value of contemplation, are you speaking of sitting and thinking over particular themes – the thirty-two parts of the body, for instance?*

ANSWER: That is not necessary when the mind is truly still. When tranquillity is properly established the right object of investigation becomes obvious. When contemplation is 'True', there is no discrimination into 'right' and 'wrong', 'good' and 'bad'; there is nothing even like that. You don't sit there thinking, 'Oh, this is like that and that is like this,' etc. That is a coarse form of contemplation. Meditative contemplation is not *merely* a matter of thinking – rather it's what we call 'contemplation in silence'. Whilst going about our daily routine we mindfully consider the real nature of existence through comparisons. This is a coarse kind of investigation but it leads to the real thing.

When you talk about contemplating the body and mind, though, do we actually use thinking? Can thinking produce true Insight? Is this vipassana?

In the beginning we need to work using thinking, even though later on we go beyond it. When we are doing true contemplation all dualistic thinking has ceased; although we need to consider dualistically to get started. Eventually all thinking and pondering comes to an end.

You say that there must be sufficient tranquillity (samadhi) to contemplate. Just how tranquil do you mean?

Tranquil enough for there to be presence of mind.

Do you mean staying with the here-and-now, not thinking about the past and future?

Thinking about the past and future is alright if you understand what these things really are, but you must not get caught up in them. Treat them the same as you would anything else – don't get caught up. When you see thinking as just thinking, then that's wisdom. Don't believe in any of it! Recognize that all of it is just something that has arisen and will cease. Simply see everything just as it is – it is what it is – the mind is the mind – it's not anything or anybody in itself. Happiness is just happiness, suffering is just suffering – it is just what it is. When you see this you will be beyond doubt.

I still don't understand. Is true contemplating the same as thinking?

We use thinking as a tool, but the knowing that arises because of its use is above and beyond the process of thinking; it leads to our not being fooled by our thinking any more. You recognize that all thinking is merely the movement of the mind, and also that the knowing is not born and doesn't die. What do you think all this movement called 'mind' comes out of? What we talk about as the mind – all the activity – is just the conventional mind. It's not the real mind at all. What is real just IS, it's not arising and it's not passing away.

Trying to understand these things just by talking about them, though, won't work. We need to really consider impermanence, unsatisfactoriness and impersonality (*anicca, dukkha, anatta*); that is, we need to use thinking to contemplate the nature of conventional reality. What comes out of this work is wisdom; and if it's real wisdom everything's completed, finished – we recognize emptiness. Even though there may still be thinking, it's empty – you are not affected by it.

How can we arrive at this stage of the real mind?

You work with the mind you already have, of course! See that all that arises is uncertain, that there is nothing stable or substantial. See it clearly and see that there is really nowhere to take a hold of anything – it's all empty.

When you see the things that arise in the mind for what they are, you won't have to work with thinking any more. You will have no doubt whatsoever in these matters.

To talk about the 'real mind' and so on, may have a relative use in helping us understand. We invent names for the sake of study, but actually nature just is how it is. For example, sitting here downstairs on the stone floor. The floor is the base – it's not moving or going anywhere. Upstairs, above us is what has arisen out of this. Upstairs is like everything that we see in our minds: form, feeling, memory, thinking. Really, they don't exist in the way we presume they do. They are merely the conventional mind. As soon as they arise, they pass away again; they don't really exist in themselves.

There is a story in the scriptures about Venerable Sariputta examining a bhikkhu before allowing him to go off wandering (*dhutanga vatta*). He asked him how he would reply if he was questioned, 'What happens to the Buddha after he dies?' The bhikkhu replied, 'When form, feeling, perception, thinking and consciousness arise, they pass away.' Venerable Sariputta passed him on that.

Practice is not just a matter of talking about arising and passing away, though. You must *see* it for yourself. When you are sitting, simply see what is actually happening. Don't follow anything. Contemplation doesn't mean being caught up in thinking. The contemplative thinking of one on the Way is not the same as the thinking of the world. Unless you understand properly what is meant by contemplation, the more you think the more confused you will become.

The reason we make such a point of the cultivation of mindfulness is because we need to see clearly what is going on. We must understand the processes of our hearts. When such mindfulness and understanding are present, then everything is taken care of. Why do you think one who knows the Way never acts out of anger or delusion? The causes for these things to arise are simply not there. Where would they come from? Mindfulness has got everything covered.

Is this mind you are talking about called the 'Original Mind'?

What do you mean?

It seems as if you are saying there is something else outside of the conventional body-mind (five khandha). Is there something else? What do you call it?

There isn't anything and we don't call it anything – that's all there is to it! Be finished with all of it. Even the knowing doesn't belong to anybody, so be finished with that, too! Consciousness is not an individual, not a being, not a self, not an other, so finish with that – finish with everything! There is nothing worth wanting! It's all just a load of trouble. When you see clearly like this then everything is finished.

Could we not call it the 'Original Mind'?

You can call it that if you insist. You can call it whatever you like, for the sake of conventional reality. But you must understand this point properly. This is very important. If we didn't make use of conventional reality we wouldn't have any words or concepts with which to consider actual reality – Dhamma. This is very important to understand.

What degree of tranquillity are you talking about at this stage? And what quality of mindfulness is needed?

You don't need to go thinking like that. If you didn't have the right amount of tranquillity you wouldn't be able to deal with these questions at all. You need enough stability and concentration to know what is going on – enough for clarity and understanding to arise.

Asking questions like this shows that you are still doubting. You need enough tranquillity of mind to no longer get caught in doubting what you are doing. If you had done the practice you would understand these things. The more you carry on with this sort of questioning, the more confusing you make it. It's all right to talk if the talking helps contemplation, but it won't show you the way things actually are. This Dhamma is not understood because somebody else tells you about it, you must see it for yourself – *paccattaṁ*.

If you *have* the quality of understanding that we have been talking about, then we say that your duty to do anything is over; which means that you don't *do* anything. If there is still something to do, then it's your duty to do it.

Simply keep putting everything down, and know that that is what you are doing. You don't need to be always checking up on yourself, worrying about things like 'How much *samadhi*' – it will always be the right amount. Whatever arises in your practice, let it go; know it all as uncertain, impermanent. Remember that! It's all uncertain. Be finished with all of it. This is the Way that will take you to the source – to your Original Mind.

AJAHN SUMEDHO

Ajahn Sumedho (Robert Jackman) was born in Seattle, Washington in 1934. On graduating from university, he joined the U.S. Navy as a medical officer and served in the Korean War. Returning to academic life, he took an M.A. in South Asian Studies from the University of California (Berkeley) in 1963. After a short spell working for the Red Cross, he went out to the Far East and spent two years teaching English with the Peace Corps in Borneo.

His growing interest in Buddhism took him (in 1966) to Thailand, where he sought to enter monastic life. He became a novice in Nong Khai and a bhikkhu one year later in 1967, with Chao Khun Rajapreechayamuni as preceptor. Soon after his ordination, he was taken to meet Ajahn Chah, with whom he stayed and trained for ten years. Following a *tudong* pilgrimage in India in 1974, he helped establish Wat Pah Nanachat and became its abbot.

In 1977 Ajahn Chah was invited by the English Sangha Trust to visit Britain. He brought Ajahn Sumedho with him, and seeing the interest there, left him in London (at the Hampstead Vihara) in charge of a small group of bhikkhus. In 1979 the monks were able to move to Sussex, which marked the beginning of Chithurst Buddhist Monastery. Interest flourished, and under Ajahn Sumedho's guidance Amaravati Buddhist Centre near London was established in 1984, in addition to branch monasteries in the north and south-west of England, and also in Switzerland and New Zealand.

In 1981 Ajahn Sumedho was appointed an *Upajjhaya* (preceptor). He was also president (1983-87) of the London-based Buddhist Society.

THE WAY IT IS

The following teaching is taken from the first two talks given by Venerable Ajahn Sumedho to the monastic community of Amaravati during the winter retreat of 1988.

The mind of an enlightened human being is flexible; the mind of an ignorant person is fixed.

TODAY IS THE FULL MOON OF JANUARY and the beginning of our winter retreat. We can have an all-night meditation sitting tonight to commemorate the auspiciousness of the occasion. It's very fortunate to have an opportunity such as this to devote ourselves for two months to one-pointed reflection on Dhamma.

The teaching of the Buddha is the understanding of The Way Things Are – being able to look, to be awake. It means developing attentiveness, brightness, and wisdom – developing the Eightfold Path, which we call *bhavana*.

Now when we're reflecting on things as they are, we're 'seeing', rather than interpreting through a veil of self-view. The big obstacle all of us have to face is this insidious belief in the 'I am' – attachment to self-view. It's so ingrained in us that we're like fish in the water: water is so much a part of the fish's life that it doesn't notice it. The sensory world we've been swimming in since our birth is like that for us. If we don't take time to observe it for what it really is then we'll die without getting any the wiser.

But this opportunity as a human being has the great advantage for us of our being able to reflect – we can reflect on the water we're swimming in. We can observe the sensory realm for what it is. We're not trying to get rid of it. We're not complicating it by trying to add to it – we're just being aware of it as it is. We're no longer deluding ourselves by appearances, by fears, desires and all the things we create in our mind about it.

This is what we mean when we use such terms like: 'It is as it is.' If you ask someone who is swimming in water, 'What is water like?', then they simply bring attention to it and say, 'Well, it feels like *this*. It's *this* way.' Then you ask, 'How is it *exactly*? Is it wet or cold or warm or hot...?' All of these words can describe it. Water can be cold, warm, hot, pleasant, unpleasant... But it's just like *this*. The sensory realm we're swimming in for a lifetime is **this way**! It feels like **this**! You feel it! Sometimes it's pleasant. Sometimes it's unpleasant. Most of the time it's neither pleasant nor unpleasant. But always it's just *this* way. Things come and go and change, and there's nothing that you can depend on as being totally stable. The sensory realm is all energy and change and movement; all flux and flow. Sensory consciousness is this way.

Now we're not judging it; we're not saying it's good or it's bad, or you should like it, or you shouldn't; we're just bringing attention to it – like the water. The sensory realm is a realm of feeling. We are born into it and we feel it. From the time the umbilical cord is severed we're physically independent beings; we're no longer physically tied to anybody else. We feel hunger; we feel pleasure; we feel pain, heat, and cold. As we grow, we feel all kinds of things. We feel with the eyes, the ears, the nose, the tongue, the body; and with the mind itself. There is the ability to think and remember, to perceive and conceive. All this is feeling. It can be lots of fun and wonderful, but it can also be depressing, mean and miserable; or it can be neutral – neither pleasant nor painful. So all sensory impingement is The Way It Is. Pleasure is *this* way; pain is *this* way. The feeling of neither pleasure nor pain is *this* way.

To be able to truly reflect on these things, you have to be alert and attentive. Some people think that it is up to me to tell them how it is: 'Ajahn Sumedho, how should I be feeling right now?' But we're not *telling* anybody how it is; we're *being* open and receptive to how it is. There's no need to tell someone how it is when they can find out for themselves. So this two months of finding out how it is, is a valuable opportunity. Many human beings it seems, are not even aware that such a development of wisdom is possible.

What do we mean when we use this word wisdom? From birth to death, this is **the way it is**. There's always going to be a certain amount of pain, and discomfort, unpleasantness and ugliness.

And if we're not aware of it as it really is – see it as *Dhamma* – then we tend to create a problem out of it. The span between birth and death becomes all very personal; it becomes fraught with all kinds of fears and desires and complications.

We suffer a lot in our society from loneliness. So much of our life is an attempt to not be lonely: 'Let's talk to each other; let's do things together so we won't be lonely.' And yet inevitably, we are really alone in these human forms. We can pretend; we can entertain each other; but that's about the best we can do. When it comes to the actual experience of life, we're very much alone; and to expect anyone else to take away our loneliness is asking too much.

When there's physical birth, notice how it makes us seem separate. We're not physically joined to each other, are we? With attachment to this body we feel separate and vulnerable; we dread being left alone and we create a world of our own that we can live in. We have all kinds of interesting companions: imaginary friends, physical friends, enemies, but the whole lot of it comes and goes, begins and ends. Everything is born and dies in our own minds. So we reflect that birth conditions death. Birth and death; beginning and ending.

During this retreat, this kind of reflection is highly encouraged: contemplate what birth is. Right now we can say: 'This is the result of being born; this body. It's like *this*: it's conscious and it feels, there's intelligence, there's memory, there's emotion.' All these can be contemplated because they are mind objects; they are dhammas. If we attach to the body as a subject, or to opinions and views and feelings as 'me' and 'mine', then we feel loneliness and despair; there's always going to be the threat of separation and ending. Attachment to mortality brings fear and desire into our lives. We can feel anxious and worried even when life is quite all right. So long as there's ignorance – *avijja* – regarding the true nature of things, fear is always going to dominate consciousness.

But anxiety is not ultimately true. It's something we create. Worry is just *that much*. Love and joy and all the best in life, if we are attached to them, are going to bring the opposite along also. That's why in meditation we practise accepting the feeling of these things. When we accept things for what they are, we're no longer attached to them. They just are what they are; they arise and cease, they're not a self.

Now from the perspective of our cultural background, how does it appear? Our society tends to reinforce the view that everything is 'me' and 'mine'. 'This body is me; I look like this; I am a man; I am an American; I am 54 years old; I am an abbot.' But these are just conventions, aren't they? We're not saying I'm not these things; rather we're observing how we tend to complicate them by believing in the 'I am'. If we attach to them, life becomes so much more than it actually is; it becomes like a sticky web. It gets so complicated; whatever we touch sticks to us. And the longer we live the more complicated we make it. So much fear and desire comes from that commitment to 'I am' – to being somebody. Eventually they take us to anxiety and despair; life seems much more difficult and painful than it really is.

But when we just observe life for what it is, then it's all right: the delights, the beauty, the pleasures, are *just that.* The pain, the discomfort, the sickness, are what they are. We can always cope with the way life moves and changes. The mind of an enlightened human being is flexible and adaptable. The mind of the ignorant person is conditioned and fixed.

Whatever we fix on is going to be miserable. Being a man, or being a woman, as a permanent belief, is always going to make life difficult. Any class we identify with – middle class, working class, American, British, Buddhist, Theravadin Buddhist – grasping to any of these will produce some kind of complication, frustration and despair.

Yet conventionally, one can be all these things – a man, an American, a Buddhist, a Theravadin; these are merely perceptions of mind. They are adequate for communication; but they're nothing more than that. They're what is called *sammuttidhamma* – 'conventional reality'. When I say, 'I'm Ajahn Sumedho,' that's not a self, not a person; it's a convention. Being a Buddhist monk is not a person – it's a convention; being a man is not a person, it's a convention. Conventions are as they are. When we attach to them out of ignorance, we become bound and limited. That's the sticky web! We're blinded; being deluded by the convention.

When we let go of the conventions, we don't throw them away. I don't have to kill myself or disrobe; the conventions are all right. There's no suffering involved in any of these if there is the awakened mind seeing them for what they are; they just are as they are. They're merely a convenience; expedient to time and place.

With the realization of 'ultimate reality' (*paramatthadhamma*), there is the freedom of Nibbana. We are free from the delusions of desire and fear; this freedom from conventions is the Deathless. But to realize this we have to really look at what attachment is. What is it all about? What is suffering, and attachment to the 'I am' process? What is it? We're not asking anybody to deny themselves; attachment to the view of being nobody is *still* somebody. It's not a matter of affirmation or negation but of realization; of seeing. To do this we use mindfulness.

With mindfulness we can open to the totality. In the beginning of this retreat, we open to the whole two months. On the first day, we've already accepted in full awareness all possibilities: sickness and health, success and failure, happiness and suffering, enlightenment or total despair. We're not thinking, 'I'm only going to get . . . , I only want to have . . . , I want to have only the nice things happen to me. And I've got to protect myself so that I'll have an idyllic retreat; be perfectly safe and tranquillized for two months.' That in itself is a miserable state, isn't it? Instead, we take all the possibilities, from the best to the worst. And we're doing this consciously. That means: everything that happens during these two months is part of the retreat – it's a part of our practice. The Way Things Are is Dhamma for us: happiness and suffering, enlightenment or total despair – *everything!*

If we practise this way, then despair and anguish take us to calm and peace. When I was in Thailand I had a lot of these negative states – loneliness, boredom, anxiety, doubt, worry and despair. But accepted as they are, they cease. And what's left when there's no more despair?

The Dhamma that we're looking at now, is subtle. Not subtle in the sense that it's high up – it's so ordinary, so very much here and now that we don't notice it. Just like the water for the fish. Water is so much a part of its life the fish doesn't notice it; even though it's swimming in it. Sensory consciousness is here, now. It's *this* way. It's not distant. It's not really difficult. It's just a matter of paying attention to it. The way out of suffering is the way of mindfulness: mindful-awareness or wisdom.

So we keep bringing our attention to the way things are. If you have nasty thoughts, or feel resentful, bitter or irritated, then notice what it feels like in your heart. If we're frustrated and angry during this time, it's all right because we've already allowed for that to happen. It's a part of the practice; it's the way things are. Remember, we're not trying to become angels and saints – we're not trying to get rid of all our impurities and coarseness and just be happy. The human realm is like **this**! It can be very coarse and it can be pure. Pure and impure are a pair. To know purity and impurity is mindfulness-wisdom. To know that impurity is impermanent and not-self is wisdom. But the minute we make it personal – 'Oh, I shouldn't have impure thoughts!' – we're stuck again in the realm of despair. The more we try to have only pure thoughts, the more the impure thoughts keep coming. That way we make sure we're going to be miserable for the whole two months; guarantee it. Out of ignorance we create a realm for ourselves that can only be miserable.

So in mindfulness, or full-mindedness, all misery and all happiness are of equal value: no preferences. Happiness is **this** way. Misery is **this** way. They arise and they cease. Happiness is still happiness; it's not misery. And misery is still misery; it's not happiness. But it is what it is. And it's nobody's and it's only **that much**. And we don't suffer from it. We accept it, we know it and we understand it. All that arises ceases. All dhamma is not self.

So I offer this for your reflection.

VENERABLE SANTACITTO

Venerable Santacitto (Stephen Saslav) was born of Jewish parents in Brooklyn, New York City in 1947. He excelled at mathematics in high school and went on to study at university.

In 1967, just after the Six Day War, he went to Israel to work on a kibbutz. Continuing but not completing his university studies in Jerusalem, he left and went hitch-hiking through Africa, where he was drawn to climb Mount Kilimanjaro in Tanzania. Travelling on through the Seychelles, India and Nepal, he ended up working as an English teacher in Bangkok, where he took a meditation course with Sister Sudhamma. Through her he met an American disciple of Ajahn Chah, Dr. Douglas Burns, whose clever persuasion induced him to visit Wat Pah Pong. Although he was unable to speak Thai, he was deeply affected by meeting Ajahn Chah and Ajahn Sumedho, recognizing in them the self-actualization that had profoundly inspired him in Abraham Maslow's book, *Toward a Psychology of Being*.

The existence of a path to self-actualization motivated him to become a samanera for a short experimental period. Finding himself unable to leave, however, he went on to receive *upasampada* in 1971 at Wat Benjamabopitr under Chao Khun Buddhivongsamuni. His twelve years in Thailand were punctuated by seven months back in Brooklyn, and nine months in France. In 1985, at Ajahn Sumedho's invitation, he moved to Amaravati in England, where he established the multi-faith Christmas Humphreys Memorial Library, and was instrumental in setting up an exhibition on lay people's practice in 1988.

He is now senior incumbent of the Devon Vihara.

LOVE AND ATTACHMENT

The following teaching has been adapted from a session of questions and answers which took place during a retreat led by Venerable Santacitto at Amaravati, September 1988.

Probably the easiest way to outgrow ourselves is through the response of compassionate action.

QUESTION: *Could you speak on the differences and similarities of love and compassion?*

ANSWER: Compassion is a sensitivity to the experience of suffering, or *dukkha*: a sensitivity of heart to the suffering of others. It's a 'non-separation' from our own heart's response on sensing suffering in another. And because it is a kind of suffering in itself, it impels action. However, since it's not a suffering arising out of selfishness – that is, from our own sense of separateness – it doesn't impel blind action. In taking one beyond oneself, the experience of compassion is a very powerful opportunity for the arising and development of wisdom. Probably the easiest way to outgrow ourselves is through the response of compassionate action.

Love is a more directly positive quality. With a positive response of heart we thoroughly accept another's reality, with an acceptance that encompasses any resistance we might feel. Again there is the sense of 'non-separation', but this time it is in relationship to happiness.

With love, because it often involves highly positive feelings, one can easily become lost in it. Hence we have the expression, 'Love blinds.' Compassion, being more in touch with suffering, tends to keep us grounded better than the sometimes eruptive energies involved in love. One can see how, without care and attention, love can easily drift from being a selfless sensitivity, to becoming an attachment. It slowly becomes 'self-interested'.

The best example of selfless love – and we are all familiar with it – is the self-sacrificing love of a mother for her child. But it is also a good example of how attachment creeps in. In its original purity of complete acceptance, love is an extremely pleasant experience. But unless we are very clear about feelings of 'getting something out of it', attachment does slowly creep in. And where attachment arises, love is blocked. By limiting our acceptance, the completeness of love disappears.

Though compassion mightn't be as conducive to attachment as love, 'self' can still get involved if we are not careful. That which might have been compassion to begin with can turn into pity – 'feeling sorry for someone' – which doesn't bridge the sense of separateness. Looking down on others doesn't help us grow beyond ourselves.

If we make the effort to intentionally cultivate love, we find it's a quality that can be directed towards all people, including those who we don't necessarily even consider friends. In such cases, rather than feeling euphoric ecstasy, we experience a simple kindness, a sort of grandheartedness – a willingness to coexist.

We must remember, however, that talking about 'pure love' and 'pure compassion' is not with the idea of creating *absolutes,* but to help guide us in our practice. By recollecting in this way, we can come to appreciate how, the less we allow personal gain to become mixed in, the more all beings benefit.

Is devotion another kind of love? Can it be a form of cultivating love?

Yes; I would say the experiences of devotion and love are very similar. We could say, devotion is a love directed towards someone for whom we feel respect. It includes a sense of gratitude also for the benefits that we have received.

Would you say that it's possible to experience a devotional heart quality without a human being as the object – maybe towards a tree?

Yes; and there also you are feeling gratitude for what the tree gives you by its existence.

When I see nature, I am so full of gratitude, but that seems to be a kind of attachment. I try to see the attachment, but it's difficult. Someone once told me: 'If you go on like this, you will never be free.' [Laughter] I just love trees and birds and nature... and I find I'm having to change... I don't know how to deal with it.

It's true that some of these positive qualities of heart may come under the classification of 'attachments', but they can be pretty darned healthy attachments. I sometimes like to look at the practice path as being similar to climbing a ladder; so long as what we're holding on to doesn't obstruct our ability to pull ourselves further upwards, then a so-called attachment might be serving a useful function. However, if we're holding on to a higher rung of the ladder but won't let go of a lower one, then we're stuck. We've got a problem. So holding on to something that is keeping us from going on, even if it's pleasurable, is blocking progress.

Yes, but I'm not sure that I want enlightenment to be like that. [Laughter]

Eventually, we have to let go of everything – but in the right time. We shouldn't try to *force* ourselves to let go of things! It's just that from time to time life happens to present us with opportunities where we can either let go or not let go.

Is 'letting go' a necessary part of meditation?

It's entirely up to the individual. There is no need to feel that you have to let go of your devotion towards nature. But later on, you may begin to sense something more valuable in your life, the development of which could be aided by a more balanced relationship with nature. For example, you may begin to feel a greater need for the power of equanimity, finding that always gushing outwards towards nature is something that is preventing you from further blossoming. So you may realize that equanimity need not be a negation or rejection. It's more a matter of allowing the appreciation of nature to settle to a deeper level. It's starting to recognize the nature within ourselves as well as the nature 'out there'.

Generally though, as far as trees are concerned, I would say they are a rung of the ladder which pulls us up; especially in our modern materialistic society. To a large extent we have lost touch with our ability to really *be with* nature. We've forgotten how it functions to help us tune in to our inner nature. Remembering that, simply being with nature can be a very beautiful stepping-up point. Appreciating trees and birds and external nature, definitely doesn't have to be an obstacle to get rid of. We can learn to use such appreciation as a point of balance in our lives – not only for ourselves, but to share with others also. This is something we need a lot of.

It's so sad to hear people always complaining about everything. If only they would just walk outside. . . .

Yes, we tend to get lost into our personal space and limit the mind. Just walking outside and opening up can be a way of letting things free.

Do you think that there is symbolic meaning to the Buddha's getting enlightened under a tree? Maybe it means that we can learn from nature. Trees can teach us how to refine ourselves. We can come to understand how important it is to give back to nature what has been taken away.

That is a very good point; the Buddha was born under a tree, enlightened under a tree, and died under a tree. And he said that sitting under trees was a good thing to do. His recommendation to his bhikkhus was: 'There are these trees, go, sit.'

Our particular monastic tradition here comes from what is known as the 'forest tradition' of Thailand. There's an emphasis in this tradition which says that if one really wishes to practise under ideal conditions, then the forests provide these conditions. In their simplicity we can discover an invaluable reflection of our inner nature.

To a large extent, Ajahn Chah's teachings were influenced by his vast experience of living in forests. Many of the similes that he used came out of this. His own practice was simply a matter of being a totally open and aware human being in natural surroundings, watching both inwardly and outwardly to see what was happening. Out of such practice came a very deep understanding of himself. But he wasn't trapped by nature. When he needed to go to the city, he could do that quite comfortably without yearning for the forests. He could make the most out of the forest, without becoming dependent upon it. If we become attached to being in the forests – as monks sometimes do – then that's a sign that there's still something to learn from nature.

VENERABLE PABHAKARO

Venerable Pabhakaro (Gordon Kappel) was born in Seattle, Washington in 1948. He joined the U.S. Army in 1967 and was sent to Vietnam in 1969, where as a captain in the 1st Cavalry Division (Air Mobile) he piloted helicopters. He came into contact with Buddhism while on rest-and-relaxation (R&R) in Bangkok, where he visited several monasteries and met some of the Western monks living there.

In 1970 he was sent back to the U.S., to Alabama, where he began seriously studying Buddhism, lived by the eight precepts and began experimenting with teaching himself meditation. Having decided he wanted to become a bhikkhu, he applied for and was granted an honourable discharge from the service on conscientious grounds. On returning to Thailand he became a novice a Wat Bovornives, and in due course received bhikkhu ordination at Wat Pah Pong in 1972.

When Ajahn Sumedho left for England in 1977, Venerable Pabhakaro took over as senior monk at Wat Pah Nanachat until he himself went with Ajahn Chah to Europe and the U.S. on a visit in 1979. On returning to Thailand he spent an 18-month period walking on *tudong* and living in solitude, before going back to live with Ajahn Chah, whose health was deteriorating. As one of Ajahn Chah's principle nursing attendants, he took responsibility for setting up a purpose-built clinic at Wat Pah Pong.

Venerable Pabhakaro went to England in 1984 and assisted with the establishment of Amaravati Buddhist Centre. He is currently the senior incumbent at Harnham Vihara, and was featured recently in the TVS television programme 'Almsbowls to Newcastle'.

ON HUMILITY

The following teaching is adapted from a talk given by Venerable Pabhakaro during a retreat in Scotland in August 1988.

Ultimately, what we are bowing to is the highest human potentials – peace, love and understanding.

WHEN WE STOP TO INVESTIGATE THE TEACHINGS, we can see the importance of personal responsibility: of taking responsibility for what we do, what we say, and eventually for what we think. We see the possibility of developing something – of cultivating our body, speech and mind. I personally felt very attracted to this way particularly because there was room to doubt and question. I was very inspired by the thought of not having to take anything on board just because it was written down; one was being encouraged to explore through meditation and self-enquiry.

Now I'm in the position where I have the opportunity to share my experience; to teach. The way I was taught and trained was to open in the present moment, to the best of one's ability, and speak from the heart – to speak from one's own experience. My intention is to make an offering. Sometimes this feels comfortable and one is very confident. At other times I have to question and reconsider: maybe that's not what people need or what they can relate to. In such questioning I always try to come back to this intention and to look with an attitude of openness and honesty, asking myself: 'Where am I coming from?'

Honesty to me seems to be one of the most beneficial things that we as human beings can develop. It is one of the Buddhist Perfections – *sacca parami* – truthfulness or honesty. Whether we consider ourselves spiritual or religious or not, if we aren't honest with ourselves then there is a deception that we pass on to others. It may be very subtle, but if we deceive ourselves, how can we not deceive others?

When I try to be honest I feel humble. There is a feeling of meekness and sinking down with humility. Now, reflecting on these words, in popular culture we sometimes say that humiliation is one of the most degrading experiences we can have – 'That was one of the most humiliating experiences of my life' – which is very negative. In one sense it is the lowest of the low to be put down . physically or verbally; especially verbally, as something someone says can make us feel degraded and belittled. Usually the feeling that comes up when this happens is revenge: 'I've been made a fool of, I'll get them!' What is really happening in that situation is that ego is being threatened. All our defence mechanisms are triggered into a kind of red alert to defend ourselves.

In the religious life, however, we talk about 'developing' a quality of humility, because, by taking a positive attitude towards it, we can turn situations around and grow from them. Maybe you question this, thinking: 'Wouldn't this make us weak and servile?' But it's not to say that we have to let everybody walk all over us: that we lie prone on the street and let people trample on us so we can be humiliated and therefore become humble. Rather we see how we can refrain from reacting or over-reacting in situations by learning to lay down our pride and opinions.

Consider what happens if we don't react when someone verbally attacks us. What they're usually looking for is some sort of reaction that they can feed on. It's like practising tennis and hitting a ball against a wall; you can do it because there's a reaction. If someone throws verbal abuse at us and we don't react with aversion, aggression, or anything, but just absorb it, then it deflates and fizzles out. When this happens in our daily-life situations, try to see how we can move towards not-reacting by just being able to absorb.

I try to practise this when I travel, although it's not usually verbal abuse that I receive – even though people can sometimes yell something once you've passed by. It's a more subtle physical reaction that one feels, an aggressive energy that you sense when people walk by. When this happens, my instinctive reaction is to meet it with aggression, but what I try to practise is simply absorbing that aggressiveness. It's incredible what this different attitude does to one's physical and mental state. It changes from a tightening of the abdomen with clenched fists ready for defence, to a softening and absorbing reception. So this is a way of learning to use these situations and energies skilfully. It results in a feeling of humility.

Most of my life I've been amongst the biggest and the strongest, having to live up to an image of being six foot three and weighing 200 pounds, so there's never been the problem like the wee lads had of always trying to prove themselves. Softening that image felt very foreign, especially when everything inside me was saying: 'Puff out your chest, bulge out your arms and be a man.' But whether we're large, middling or small, practising like this is difficult.

This is why I find the religious form a very beautiful thing to have. It gives one a skilful means to work with. We have devotional practices like bowing and chanting. Of these, one of the most difficult is bowing. No matter what we bow towards, it doesn't come naturally for us; there's a great deal of resistance to doing it. A lot of it comes from our conditioning about bowing to idols. But really, what is it that doesn't want to bow?

In my own practice I recognized quite early on this resistance to bowing. I was fortunate in meeting Venerable Ajahn Chah, a man whom I considered to be a genuine Master. It was quite easy to humble myself and bow at his feet. Not because he said: 'Bow at my feet,' but because that was the form and I wanted to do it. It was so nice to take this large frame and prostrate it on the ground instead of standing tall, thinking: 'Hey! look at me; ain't I tough. Big Mean ME.' I felt a softening take place, and putting it on the ground brought a great joy into my heart.

Those not familiar with our way may find it difficult to understand. In Western culture we tend to form strong opinions, often judging immediately by the appearance of things. Visitors come to the monastery and see those who have been around for a number of years bowing and acting in a humble way, and may think that we systematically brain-wash people and are out to boost our egos. It might look like we have whipped and beaten them into doing these things and they appear to be servile. To be honest, when people actually bow to me – as is the Thai custom – it brings up a feeling of wanting to lower myself in a similar way, so I bow in return with my heart. It's like the hand gesture of *añjali* (bringing one's palms together) which comes from the Indian tradition and means *Namaste*: 'I revere the Highest or Divinity within you.' Here in the West, especially America, you hold out your hand and give the other guy's paw a big squeeze: 'How are ya! Glad to meet ya!' Now I find *añjali* a nicer gesture.

A number of years ago we had an English Tibetan nun staying with us at Ajahn Chah's home monastery in Thailand. One evening Ajahn Chah went over to the nuns' community to offer a teaching. He asked me to come along in order to do the translating for her benefit. After he had finished talking and I had translated, we stayed on for a while answering questions. Earlier in the day, Ajahn Chah had observed the nun as she was circumambulating the main Uposatha Hall doing full-length Tibetan-style prostrations. He now asked her if she would demonstrate it for us and the other nuns. After agreeing, she stood up, requesting plenty of room, and explained each action as she went along.

She showed how the hand gesture meant an offering of first one's body, then speech, and finally one's mind. Continuing, she moved her arms out to the side and over the head in a wide sweeping motion, symbolizing the inclusion of all sentient beings in the act. Once she was completely prone on the floor, the arms and hands did a sweeping motion one more time, with the hands finishing over the back of the head directed skywards in *añjali*. As she lay prone for the second time and her hands came over the head in the final gesture, Ajahn Chah pointed and exclaimed: 'That is surrender!' I'll never forget that. He was emphasizing the beauty in the physical gesture of 'I give up. I surrender.' If seen with proper understanding, it's the most humble bodily expression of human devotion. Even the most proud and ego-centred person cannot deny that.

So in the monastery I can be a stickler for training the new monks in proper bowing, and have been known on occasions to give people a hard time for not doing it correctly. We train in it because it's a way of stopping: taking time to collect and compose ourselves, learning to put our hearts into it. Ultimately what we are bowing to is not a golden image but that which it symbolizes – the highest human potentials of peace, love and understanding.

Each night before I bed down I bow six times and again first thing on arising. It doesn't matter where I am, I still do it. When I stay in people's houses I still bow, which is always an interesting reflection if the room they offer me has posters on the walls of celebrities like Boy George. Whether there is an image of the Buddha or not makes little difference if we are humbling ourselves to the Highest Quality within. This is something that each of us can work on.

Whether we wish to use these forms and traditions or not is our own choice. They are here for our benefit to be used skilfully. When I notice people not bowing I don't get upset, I just feel a bit of sadness. When I see you doing it this brings a good feeling to my heart. I know how difficult it is, but because you are willing to work with it, it's very uplifting. This is what makes the struggle of cultivating humility worth our effort.

VENERABLE KHEMADHAMMO

Venerable Khemadhammo (Alan Adams) was born in Portsmouth, England in 1944, and trained at drama school to become an actor. In his seven-year acting career he travelled worldwide (including a 14,000-mile tour of the U.S.) and spent three years with the National Theatre Company. Becoming interested in Buddhism, he eventually decided to go to Thailand to become a bhikkhu.

In 1971 he became a samanera at Wat Mahathat with Tan Chao Khun Demp Siddhumani. One year later he went to Wat Pah Pong, and received *upasampada* (1972). He accompanied Ajahn Chah and Ajahn Sumedho to England in 1977, taking up residence at the Hampstead Vihara. During this time he developed an interest in working with prisoners, which Ajahn Chah encouraged. This work has developed steadily over the years, and in 1984 Venerable Khemadhammo formed a Buddhist prison chaplaincy organization, 'Angulimala'. Officially recognized by the Home Office, its patrons include Venerable Dr. Saddhatissa, Venerable Sangharakshita, Ajahn Sumedho and Lord Avebury.

Venerable Khemadhammo spent five years at a vihara which he founded on the Isle of Wight, during which time he featured in the BBC television documentary 'In More Ways Than One'. In 1985 he moved to his current residence, the Forest Hermitage, in Warwick shire. A stupa was built there in 1988, known as the 'English Shwe Dagon'. Presently he lives with several other bhikkhus, continuing to visit prisons, teach meditation, and lecture regularly on Buddhism for Warwick University's Open University Programme.

RESPONDING TO PAIN

This article was prepared by Venerable Khemadhammo at the request of 'Caduceus' magazine and appeared in their December 1987 issue.

**Insight practice uses everything;
it turns everything to an advantage.**

PAIN AND SUFFERING ARE ONLY TOO WELL KNOWN
to require much of an introduction. Suffering describes the
experience of varying degrees of discomfort, and pain is the
alarm which forces us to attend to that discomfort. Neither the
experience nor the alarm are pleasant and, naturally, we would all
prefer a world in which neither existed. The search for perfect
health, or for a system whereby perfect health might be attained,
is a response to this wish for a more satisfactory state of affairs.

Let us think of a house in which many important and valuable
objects are kept and which is equipped with the very latest
electronic alarm system. While all is left undisturbed the system
remains quiet. There may be the minor irritation of having to
check and maintain it and it may occasionally raise a false alarm,
but essentially it is silent and of no trouble to the owner. Then
suddenly, quite unexpectedly, after months or years of inactivity,
one is wrenched from one's slumber by the searing pain of bells,
sirens and flashing lights and one knows that something is wrong –
one's treasure is being plundered. How do you respond to that?
Some people turn over and go back to sleep; some reach for the
bottle, and drug themselves into oblivion; some panic; and some
quietly set about dealing with the intrusion. The last is the proper
response to pain.

Now there are two basic approaches: you can fight to get your
valuables back, the intruder captured and removed, the *status quo*
restored and the alarm reset; or you can try to accept and understand what has happened. If you only do the former, the best
you can achieve is simply to get back to where you started, but
with less security. Despite your efforts, your attachments have

been threatened and it could happen again – you've not only gained nothing, but you're losing ground. Conversely, if you choose the latter response, you're bound to benefit. You may not restore your possessions, but you will be encouraging a healthy attitude which, if fully developed, will mean that never again can alarm bells spoil your repose. Tempting, isn't it?

My Buddhist monastic training, which has included detailed contemplation of the body, has led me to have little sympathy with health regimes, special diets and the like, and in the past I've occasionally enjoyed tweaking a few attachments with dietary advice based on plenty of jam doughnuts. The Buddha has pointed out that it is sheer foolishness to claim that one's body is healthy even for a moment – in this ever-changing phenomenon, there is always something not quite right. Nevertheless, you will find that the Buddha is referred to as the 'peerless physician', whose concern is the cure of all greed, hatred, and delusion – the ending of *real* suffering.

That analogy is frequently played on and extended. At the opening ceremony of The Forest Hermitage, one of our most senior monks took it up again and compared this place to a small hospital, with myself as the house surgeon. What I am saying, then, is that there is health and Health: the former has its place, but in the long run is futile; while the latter must surely become the purpose of living.

Of course, by all means take care of your body, but reflect that whatever you do it may still be easily broken and one day it is sure to die. Of the two, a healthy mind is of much more use than a healthy body. If you're in wondrous physical shape, but your mind is disordered, you're in bad trouble. But if your body is wasted, eaten up with disease or otherwise beyond repair, and your mind is bright with wisdom, you'll be all right.

Let's go back to the analogy of the house: to sit in your house, jealously guarding its contents, polishing and improving the alarm system, equates with the ordinary health of the special diets and fitness regimes; to understand, to develop a healthy attitude, is real Health. Real Health is worthy of us. It comes through facing up to life, including pain and suffering, observing it, investigating it and comprehending its nature and its source. I think it's often obvious that those who've suffered have grown; but we must be careful, as it's not necessarily the case. It's not pain alone that generates the growth, it's how you view and use your experience. You must have the proper response – then and only then, will wisdom emerge out of suffering.

I remember being told once by an experienced burglar that he enjoyed the challenge of an elaborate alarm system; and I suspect he might also have said that where there was an alarm, he knew there was something worth having – and the more complex the alarm, the more valuable and desirable were the things to steal. Think about it: if you haven't got anything or if you have no attachment to things surrounding you, you don't need any protection. If they're there, fine; if they're not there, fine! And you sit undisturbed, content with things as they are. A healthy attitude, then, is found in a mind that has matured and grown out of desire and attachment – the mind is cool and there are no more alarms to ring. In other words, there is no more pain and suffering.

The Buddha referred to twelve kinds of suffering, which may be reduced to three, and ultimately to one. The twelve are: birth, decay, death, sorrow, lamentation, pain, grief, despair, association with the unpleasant, separation from the beloved, not to get what one desires, and the Five Aggregates. Reduced to three, there are: the ordinary suffering of aches and pains, the suffering dependent on impermanence, and the discomfort of attachment to the Five Aggregates. Reduced to one, it is conditioned existence or just the Five Aggregates that is suffering.

Most of this is quite obvious, but perhaps I'd better enlarge on these mysterious Five Aggregates, which is how Buddhism analyses a person. They are: Form, Feeling, Perception, Habitual Tendencies, and Consciousness, none of which are stable, lasting or possessed of any inherent self-hood. We sometimes refer to them as a psycho-physical process. Form obviously corresponds to the body: it is just matter, numerous particles vibrating together, in the process of becoming and breaking up, but without any ability to know an object. The remaining four – feeling, perception, habitual tendencies and consciousness – correspond to mind, and are capable of knowing an object. These Five Aggregates are all dependent on other things, and exist in interdependence with each other; as a human being, you don't have one without the others. Together they create a formation – a formation, which, like that of geese or aircraft in the sky, is continually in a state of forming as the components interact and respond to conditions.

Thus mind affects body and body affects mind. This formation arises dependent on conditions, it grows or develops according to conditions and persists where the conditions persist. For example, sight-consciousness or seeing and the pleasure or pain, perception and other mental factors that accompany a consciousness, depend on there being an object to be seen, eyes and a contact between the two. You don't see without eyes, you don't see what's behind you and you can't see anything if there's nothing to be seen. If you develop awareness and the meditation that produces insight, you will see that your world, the entire range of your experience, is just the Five Aggregates; and that suffering depends on your attachment to them – an unhealthy attitude.

Our experiential world is a complex play of these aggregates: consciousness, resting on its physical base, arises where there is an object, and is always accompanied by feeling (liking, disliking or indifference), and perception (recognizing and marking the object), as well as a variety of other habitual tendencies that *colour* the experience. This all happens so quickly that an illusion, analogous to that produced when still pictures or sound vibrations are run at a certain speed, results. This is the illusion of self.

To be aware, you will need to slow down and watch yourself carefully; then as you go on you will perceive that the phenomena that flow unceasingly before you have no intrinsic substance, are constantly on the move, and that to try to attach, grasp or reject them is bound to be frustrating. Watching the procession of thoughts, feelings and other experiences, self begins to drop out of the picture and attachment to self is correspondingly reduced. There is a shift in attitude and a disengagement. You are beginning to see things in their true nature. This insight accumulates and this is how wisdom is established. Understanding the way things are, there is contentment; you neither want them to be otherwise nor are you attached – thus, a healthy attitude.

In his first sermon, the Buddha spoke of Four Noble Truths which he had to understand fully, work with and realize before his attainment of enlightenment was complete. They are: suffering; craving, the origin of suffering; the end of suffering; and the way to realize the end of suffering. Buddhist therapy is essentially a response to suffering and the complete method includes morality, mental training and wisdom.

For us, meditation is the principal exercise in mental training, and means the process of calming and clarifying the mind. If you can imagine a precious jewel at the bottom of a lake: when the waters are turbulent, whipped up by the violence of the storm and the confusing patterns of the wind, there's no chance of your being able to look over the side of your boat and admire the brilliance of that jewel. The water's stained with mud and sand, frothing and tipping your boat this way and that, and the jewel is totally obscured. But when the storm is over and the waters have become calm, and the mud and sand has settled, then without difficulty you may pull across the lake and looking over the side, be dazzled by the luminous intensity that now shines forth unobstructed.

In the same way, the confused and turbulent mind obscures one's inherent wisdom. Of course, working with the mind is not quite as simple as the analogy of the jewel in the lake. After all, the absence of wisdom encourages the turbulent mind and we cannot afford to sit back and wait for nature to take its course and the mind to quieten of itself. But, nevertheless, the training is composed of concentration and insight, or calm and clear, which working together support each other. At the Forest Hermitage the general advice that I give is to calm the mind by concentrating on loving-kindness; followed by the practice of *vipassana*, or insight meditation, which is developed through the cultivation of mindfulness.

When sitting in meditation, you will experience pain. It may be pins and needles or aching knees, or it may be an unpleasant thought or memory. The way you use it depends on whether it is concentration or insight that you are emphasizing in your practice. In both cases the pain is recognized, but when simply trying to concentrate and calm your mind your duty is to avoid dwelling on that pain, by returning to your meditation subject with greater and more intense concentration.

Using the loving-kindness practice, it may be helpful to view the pain with loving-kindness; this softens your attitude to the pain and brings you back to your meditation subject. Your use of the pain in the concentration practice is simply as a resistance. You will appreciate that working against resistances brings energy and sharpens your attitude to whatever you are doing. Please be quite clear that this is not a case of repression – you do not try to deny your pain nor even get rid of it – you simply concentrate with greater intensity on your meditation subject, spurred on by the resistance that your pain has set up.

When developing insight, however, you use your pain by being mindful of it and watching it. The insight practice is essentially one in which a concentrated awareness is developed, with each and every experience being subject to a bare knowing. There are various techniques which help this process and it is best to familiarize yourself with such a practice, if it interests you, under proper guidance. As soon as pain is seen in this way it loses its power. Sometimes it disappears altogether, but if not, as soon as you start relating to it as just feeling, only sensations, you relax and the discomfort reduces. You then start to examine it and you will find out that it's not PAIN, not a static *thing*, but rather a shifting, ever-moving succession of experiences that flow into and out of each other. You are now on the way to realizing insight. As you work with pain in this way, so you cope with it better and you learn from it. Your pain can teach you a great deal: you will see that it is never still for an instant, that you contribute to it through your fear and dislike of it, that you even attach to it, and that lurking behind it is that ignorant mind that always wants things to be other than they are – the unhealthy attitude. Suddenly such awfulness is being turned to your advantage and you're winning.

This is the wonderful thing about insight practice; it uses everything, brings everything alive and turns everything to advantage. Whatever arises, it is your duty to observe it with bare attention. Not doing anything with it, not giving in to the mind of desire and wishing it were otherwise, but content with things as they are, mindful and watchful. In daily life too, be mindful, watchful and content. Things are as they are, they can't be otherwise. They might have been, but they're not. They are as they are. In the future it might all be different, but right now it's as it is and it's wonderful. The present is all we really have and here we will find wisdom. So give up that gaining mind, rest content, be mindful, and understanding the true nature of things, be possessed of a healthy attitude. Let go and be happy.

VENERABLE JAGARO

Venerable Jagaro (John Cianciosi) was born in Southern Italy in 1948. When he was 10 years old his family emigrated to Australia. He studied chemistry at the Melbourne Institute of Technology, but later, while working as a research chemist, he felt the need to broaden his horizons. So, like many young Australians, he set off travelling – through Bali, Indonesia and Malaysia, and ending up in Thailand, where he encountered Buddhism. He decided to become a monk and received bhikkhu ordination, aged 24, under Venerable Phra Khru Ñanasirivatana, at Wat Pleng Vipassana, in 1972.

In 1973 he moved to Wat Pah Pong to train under Ajahn Chah. In due course, he succeeded Venerable Pabhakaro as senior incumbent of Wat Pah Nanachat. At the invitation of the Buddhist Society of Western Australia, he went to Perth in 1982 with Venerable Puriso to start a monastery there. Initially, the monks lived in a house in the suburbs of Perth while a more rural setting was sought, and eventually a 97-acre site south of the city was purchased.

Venerable Jagaro, assisted by Venerable Brahmavaṁso, has since guided the development of the Bodhinyana Forest Monastery, the monks doing much of the construction of the buildings themselves. The monastic community has since grown to ten. A wide range of teaching activities are conducted at the new monastery and at the thriving Dhammaloka Buddhist Centre in Perth. Venerable Jagaro continues to visit Thailand frequently, where he is well known and respected as a teacher of Dhamma.

HAPPINESS

The following teaching by Venerable Jagaro is adapted from a Friday night Dhamma talk at the Perth Vihara, 7th June 1985, in response to the question, 'What is happiness?'

> **Through enlightenment, you gain nothing at all: the big difference is that there is real and lasting happiness.**

HAPPINESS IS SOMETHING CLOSE TO THE HEART of everybody. We all want to be happy. Happiness in the normal sense means that you always get what you want, when and how you want it. This is very difficult, because so many things are beyond our control: the weather, one's appearance, health, relationships, one's meditation – so many things we cannot control. One's striving for worldly happiness seems constantly hindered. Where is this happiness? How can we possibly be happy when everything is in this state of uncertainty and constant change? We may spend all our lives seeking it and finding disappointment. If you are a fortunate person with good conditioning and positive states of mind, you may be happy most of the time. However, there is always the opposite – when things are not as you want them to be, when the mind doesn't do what you want it to do, when people are not as you want them to be – and naturally the opposite emotions and feelings which we call unhappiness will arise. Unhappiness has to be there so long as there is happiness.

It is like Nasrudin, the wise man who acted like a fool; or maybe he was a fool who acted like a wise man. He was sitting with this big bag of little red chillies – very hot! Tears were streaming down his face and he was panting and crying and eating chillies. An old friend came by and asked, 'Nasrudin, what are you doing there eating all those really hot chillies?' Nasrudin, between gasps for air and wiping away his tears and blowing his nose, managed to say, 'I'm looking for the sweet one.'

And so we continually look for the sweet one, continually seek happiness in the conditioned, and we haven't found a sweet one yet. Even when you are getting what you want maybe you can be 90% happy, but still there is that 10% at the back of the mind that is a little bit concerned, a little bit afraid, a little bit possessive. Underneath you know it can't last! That nagging fear leads us to a spiritual path, to seek an alternative source of happiness.

In Buddhism we are striving for a different sort of happiness. Do you think there can be happiness and joy in the mind which is self-contained, independent of all conditions and perceptions, completely independent of anything whatsoever? This is the happiness of the Buddha. This is *Nibbana,* the happiness of Enlightenment and non-attachment, the happiness of no limitations, the happiness of no self.

When you stop having an invested interest in conditions and results, you are not burdened by anything. When you are not burdened the mind is at peace. It is naturally joyful and happy. The Buddha was a shining example of this happiness. From my own experiences of having met many great meditation Masters, they share this quality of inner tranquillity, despite the inability to control conditions and events.

When I went to live with Ajahn Chah, at first I was amazed, and then I was quite upset, to see how he ran his monastery. I expected him to have a really tight control over everything: keep the monks in line, keep the lay people out of the way, have a regular timetable. Ajahn Chah didn't do anything like that at all. Things would continually change in the monastery: sometimes we would meditate in the morning; sometimes we would chant; then for a month or so we would do a lot of formal practice; then we would work – continually flowing with the conditions. I began to realize that Ajahn Chah didn't go out of his way to control and regulate conditions. Everybody wanted him to have a timetable, but he just never kept to it. He would just sit there, and if people came he received them; he never turned them away. If they didn't come, then he was perfectly happy to be alone. He didn't bother to control events, yet if I have ever met a joyful happy person, it was Venerable Ajahn Chah. It wasn't that he was always laughing – although he did laugh a lot – but he just had this joy about him, whatever he was doing. He wasn't seeking anything from anybody, wasn't trying to control things in order to be happy.

In Buddhism we are interested in freedom – the freedom of non-attachment. We carry around an immense burden of attachment to everything we consider 'me' and 'mine', like a big heavy stone on our shoulders. When a wise person points out to us that we could throw off this burden, we regard them with suspicion. 'Throw it off? Then I wouldn't have anything left! I couldn't do that!' Thinking they will bring us happiness, we continue to lug around our personal investments and self interests – this great big heavy burden! The Buddha taught that nothing is worth attaching to. Do not attach to anything: that will bring true peace and happiness. Reflect on the process of what we call suffering: what it really is – how it arises. Only then can one begin to appreciate what attachment really is, what the result of attachment is, and begin to glimpse the idea and the possible results of non-attachment.

Attachment is something we create in the mind. When we let it go, we begin to experience the silent empty mind. This still, peaceful mind can be found when sitting in meditation. Is it possible to bring it also into our daily lives? Can we live as ordinary people with this non-attachment? There is one vital factor needed if we wish to live skilfully, and that factor is mindful awareness. This factor of knowing, of being present, is essential if we wish to go beyond our continual stream of thinking, projecting, analysing and reacting. It is difficult, isn't it? Without awareness, we are locked into our stale conditioning, like a monkey with its paw stuck in the biscuit jar. All it has to do to become free is let go, but this is just what it won't do. Actually, non-attachment is not something you have to do: all you have to do is stop attaching. This is natural for the enlightened mind, and it is awareness which makes this a real possibility in our lives.

The Buddha taught a Path, gave us a method of skilful means. Meditation is the tool to help us with the process of being present, of seeing attachment and tensions arising, of knowing when to relax and let go. The practice of meditation is very highly emphasized. The more you become aware, the more you can begin to experience true peace and happiness. There is no need to have anything else, no need to achieve anything.

Through Enlightenment, you gain nothing at all: all you do is get rid of the extras; you just put down your burden. Life is still life, there are still relationships, and there is still action. The big difference is that you are perfectly at peace, and there is a real and lasting happiness.

So we should all make an effort with our practice. Without meditation, life is very difficult, and progress on the spiritual path is very hard. I once knew a German who even at that time had been a monk for fifteen years, and I asked him, 'Do you still meditate?' and he said, 'Yes, I meditate regularly. I don't think it is possible to lead a spiritual life without meditation.' I have always remembered that, and I have always reflected on how true it is. Without the ability to calm the mind, without the ability to clear the mind, without the ability to sustain awareness and reflect and observe the nature of the mind and body, it is not possible to develop in the spiritual direction – the ultimate direction which enables us to let go, to stop seeking happiness from anything or anybody.

VENERABLE PASANNO

Venerable Pasanno (Reed Perry) was born in La Pas, Manitoba in Canada. He studied History at the University of Winnipeg. After graduating he spent some time travelling in India, and from there went to Thailand.

In 1974, primarily as a means to extend his stay in Thailand, he became a bhikkhu at Wat Pleng Vipassana with Phra Khru Ñanasirivatana as preceptor. However, he started to develop a genuine interest in monastic life, and during his first year as a monk was taken by his teacher to meet Ajahn Chah, with whom he asked to be allowed to stay and train.

One of the early residents of Wat Pah Nanachat, Venerable Pasanno became its abbot in his seventh year. During his incumbency Wat Pah Nanachat has developed considerably, both in physical size and in reputation, and Venerable Pasanno has become a very well known and highly respected Dhamma teacher in Thailand.

WHAT IS IMPORTANT?

This Teaching is translated from a discourse given in the Thai language by Venerable Pasanno at Buddhamonton (Buddhamandala) near Bangkok in September, 1987. It was offered during a week of formal meditation instruction and practice dedicated to His Majesty King Bhumibol on the occasion of his 60th birthday.

If we are lacking the richness of truth in our hearts, then when we die and they cremate us, our lives will be worth no more than the handful of ashes we produce.

THE BUDDHA OFFERED HIS TEACHING TO THE WORLD with the intention of showing a way to know Truth – Dhamma. His life-long gesture of renunciation was made so we could personally know this Truth. The fact that these Teachings are still with us shows that they have been put to good use by both lay and ordained people alike. It is important, however, that we understand the need for *personal* contemplation of these Teachings for their true value to arise. With such personal contemplation, if it is right, we can come to sense the completeness, coolness and calm that they offer.

As a foreigner living here in Thailand, I find life as a Buddhist monk extremely beneficial. Sometimes people visiting our monastery, Wat Nanachat, ask me how long I've been a monk. 'Over ten years,' I tell them. 'Is it good?' they like to ask. 'If it wasn't any good,' I reply, 'why would I have spent over ten years living this way? I could be doing all sorts of other things.' It is because I *personally* see the value of this Way that I live it.

Without clear understanding of the processes of our hearts, we create all kinds of problems. We become hot and bothered and are dragged about by emotional states. For there to be personal and global peace, these states need to be understood: the ways of the heart need to be seen clearly. This is the function and value of Dhamma.

In contemplating the Buddhist Way, it is important to see that there is absolutely no obligation or intimidation involved. Whether we take it up or not is our choice, we have complete freedom in this regard – the Buddha only offered us an introduction to the Path. There is no external judge checking up on us. He pointed out that which leads to true success, to liberation, peace and wisdom; and also that which leads to failure and confusion. No external authority is making absolute statements about what is good and bad, right and wrong, and nobody is going to punish us if our preference is not to follow. However, observe that there *is* always that within our own hearts that knows what we are doing.

So it is important that we consider together how to actually use the Buddha's Teachings and realize for ourselves their true value. We have all heard many times about the Four Noble Truths and The Eightfold Path. Maybe we have heard about them to the point where we take them for granted; we don't think they are so important any more. But these Teachings are actually referred to as 'The Heart of the Buddha's Way'. Throughout the forty-five years of his teaching the Buddha never changed or abandoned them.

Last week in our monastery I was unable to do walking meditation because I had sprained my ankle. I would join the community for the sitting period and then when it came time for walking I would go back to my hut. I made use of the time to go over some of the chanting that we do. Many times I went over the Buddha's first Discourse – the *Dhammacakkappavattana Sutta* – which contains The Four Noble Truths and the Eightfold Path. As a result I discovered many valuable points.

Let us first consider the context in which these Teachings were offered. The Buddha had spent six long years striving to see for himself the Truth. He had undergone an incredible amount of hardship – not like meditators these days, who make a lot of fuss if conditions are not exactly how they want them. When the Perfect Enlightenment eventually took place he carefully considered exactly how to go about sharing his realization. He was thirty-five years of age at the time, not old and senile – and, as he had been brought up a prince he had had the best education available. He was in the prime of his life and fully capable of articulating his understanding. So he wasn't going to hand out the Teachings to just anybody.

He decided that his five companions during the time of his asceticism were most suited. They were totally sincere in their efforts, well experienced and intelligent. He then spent several weeks walking to where they were staying. When eventually he reached them, he gave the Teachings of the Four Noble Truths and the Eightfold Path. So these Teachings are not common and insignificant.

The fact that we have heard and talked about them many times means we run the risk of their becoming mere theory for us. However, if we were to talk in a worldly sense about achieving something, we would understand that it would of course require effort; likewise in the case of the Eightfold Path. If we make the right effort then realization can take place.

Now let us consider what we mean by 'right effort'. The Buddha gave an example of throwing a stick into a river. If that stick didn't run aground on either the right bank or the left, and if it didn't sink, then it would definitely reach the sea. In terms of our practice, the left and right banks are the extremes of clinging to pleasure – *kamasukhallikanuyogo* – and clinging to pain – *attakila-mathanuyogo*. Not sinking means not relinquishing effort. If it wasn't for becoming caught in sensuality, indulging in negativity and giving up making effort, we would reach *Nibbana* – Peace. This is one of the laws of nature. A true appreciation and honest accordance with the Way shows us that it must be like that.

The Eightfold Path is called the Middle Way, which means our effort must be in the right amount. If our actions of body and speech are not in harmony with this Way; if we are getting caught up in seeking sense pleasure and really indulging in states of anger and irritability, then definitely it is impossible to see things as they actually are.

We must constantly endeavour to make the right kind of effort or we will end up like the stick, and sink. When we are feeling enthusiastic we can easily give ourselves to the practice. But it can also happen that at times we are totally disillusioned, even to the extent that we forget completely the original confidence and faith we had. But that is natural. It is like swimming a long way; we become tired. We don't need to panic; simply be still for a while. Then when we have regained strength, continue. Just don't sink! Understand that much: in accordance with nature, that state will change. Despair, if that is what has arisen, will pass. Just keep practising. Observing our minds and seeing how our attitudes are continually changing shows us that impermanence is natural.

Understand how necessary this kind of contemplation of Dhamma is in our lives. It is like nourishment to the heart. If we don't have clear understanding, then it is as if something is missing. Often people who visited Ajahn Chah would say they didn't have time to practise. They'd say they had too many commitments. He would ask them: 'Do you have enough time to breathe?' They always replied, 'Oh yes! It's natural to breathe.'

Isn't cultivating Dhamma as important as breathing? If we stop breathing then we die. If we are not established in a right understanding of the Truth of the Way Things Are, then also we die; we die from that which is truly good, from true ease and true meaning. If we are lacking the richness of truth in our hearts, then when we die and they cremate us, our lives will be worth no more than the handful of ashes we produce – and that's not much! We must investigate how to live in a way that truly accords with what the Buddha taught. Surely then we could live in harmony without conflicts, difficulties and problems to resolve.

Sila (morality) is that which shows us this Middle Way. It points to the avoidance of the extremes of pleasure and pain – it means knowing the right amount. When we live in the Middle Way regarding action of body and speech then we don't cause offence to others; we do what is appropriate for human beings. The practice of formal meditation is to train our minds and hearts to stay in the Middle Way.

These days, many people who meditate try to force their minds to be as they want them to be. They sit there arguing with their thoughts; if their attention wanders they forcibly bring it back to the breath. Too much forcing is not the Middle Way. The Middle Way is the ease that arises naturally in the mind when there is the right effort, right intention and right awareness. When practice is 'right' and there is ease of mind, we can simply watch the different states that arise and consider their nature. We don't need to argue with anything. Arguing only causes restlessness. Whatever emotion arises is within the domain of our awareness, and we simply watch. Whether it's joyful or the absolute opposite, all experiences are within the boundaries of our awareness. We just sit, watch, contemplate and recognize them; they will naturally cease. Why do they cease? Because that is their nature. It is this realization of the true nature of change that strengthens and stills the mind. With such insight (pañña) there is tranquillity (samadhi) and peace.

The Buddha's wisdom is knowing the right amount. It doesn't mean knowing everything about everything, but knowing impermanence, knowing suffering, knowing selflessness. The reason we get caught in seeing things as other than they really are is our lack of wisdom. With wisdom we know how to let go; to let go of craving, let go of clinging, let go of beliefs. We let go of the tendency to always see things in relation to a self.

What we call 'Me' is merely a convention; we were born without names. Then somebody gave us a name and after being called it for a while, we start to think that a thing called 'me and mine' actually exists. Then we feel we have to spend our lives looking after it. The wisdom of the Buddha knows how to let go of this 'self' and all that pertains to it: possessions, attitudes, views and opinions. It means letting go of the opportunity for suffering (dukkha) to arise. It means giving occasion for seeing the true nature of things.

So cultivating the Eightfold Path develops what is 'right' for human beings. Through the practice of discipline, tranquillity and wisdom (sila, samadhi, pañña) we can live in harmony. Continually being caught up in extreme states is the result of selfishness; of not knowing the right amount; of not knowing the Middle Way. This Eightfold Path is a job that we need to do. If done carefully and correctly the right result will appear.

On reciting the Buddha's First Discourse last week I was reminded of how the Eightfold Path actually takes effect. It says in the sutta: *Cakkhukarani, ñanakarani, upasamaya, abhiññaya, sambodhaya, nibbanaya samvattati.* Which means that this Path functions by opening the 'Eye of Dhamma' – *cakkhukarani*; 'giving rise to insight' – *ñanakarani*; 'giving rise to peace' – *upasamaya*; 'giving rise to knowing accurately' – *abhiññaya*; 'to knowing fully' – *sambodhaya*; and to 'realizing perfect freedom' – *nibbanaya samvattati*. This is the complete Path that the Buddha teaches. It is a Path that, when cultivated, opens the eye that sees the Dhamma, knows the Dhamma, and becomes the Dhamma. This is the eye that sees that any condition that arises also ceases.

In the scriptures we read, that when the 'Eye of Dhamma' is opened, when we see clearly the way things are, then we 'Enter the Stream of Dhamma'. It is only this knowledge that arises from the practice of the Eightfold Path which causes defilements to diminish, brings peace to the heart, and eventually frees us from all suffering. Therefore it is of supreme importance to all of us. The Eightfold Path has this function – it is something that really works.

How we practise the Buddha's Teachings depends on how we view them. It depends on what we consider as having value. Please do try to investigate and see that your lives accord with the Buddha Way.

VENERABLE ANANDO

Venerable Anando was born in Buffalo, New York in 1946, and grew up near Niagara Falls. Upon leaving high school he joined the U.S. Marines and served in Vietnam as a radio operator. Severely wounded in combat, he was flown back to the U.S., where he eventually made a remarkable recovery. Decorated and invalided out of the service, he enrolled at Buffalo University to study Psychology and French, and spent one semester at a Catholic seminary.

During this period he became disillusioned with U.S. involvement in Vietnam, and took part in the growing anti-war demonstrations, eventually deciding to go abroad again. While spending a year in France studying in Nice, he came across a book on Zen by Alan Watts, which fuelled his interest in travelling to the East. Journeying overland through Turkey and Afghanistan, he spent six months in Nepal and India, where he first encountered meditation.

In 1972, a requirement by the U.S. military that he undergo a medical checkup fortuitously took him to Thailand. While at a monastery in Pattaya, he was taken to meet Ajahn Sumedho, who was staying at Wat Kow Chalok in Chonburi. He became a samanera there, and later went to Wat Pah Pong where he took bhikkhu ordination.

After five years in Thailand, Venerable Anando went back to the U.S. in 1977 to visit his family. Instead of returning to the East, he was asked by Ajahn Chah to join Ajahn Sumedho at the Hampstead Vihara in London. Since then, he has helped establish the monasteries at Chithurst and Harnham. He is presently abbot of Chithurst Buddhist Monastery.

KINDNESS AND INSIGHT

The following talk and meditation instruction have been taken from teachings given by Venerable Anando on metta bhavana – meditation on kindness.

**'...Breathing in, being energized; breathing out,
wishing others well.'**

THERE IS A STORY IN THE SCRIPTURES (*suttas*), regarding a period in the Buddha's life about 20 years after his enlightenment. By that time the monastic community had grown quite large. And it happened that the monks living around the town of Kosambi became involved in an argument over the rules. The dispute got so intense that a schism in the community was about to form. This is something which the Buddha considered very serious indeed. Hearing of the situation he immediately went to where they were, in an attempt to re-establish peace. But each time he tried to talk with the monks they dismissed him. They told him to 'Abide in peace and inactivity here and now,' which is a euphemism for 'Get lost!'

After a few attempts at re-establishing concord in the Sangha and being dismissed or ignored, the Buddha left.

He made his way to a park where another three bhikkhu disciples were living and practising: the Venerables Anarudha, Nandiya and Kimbila. Now these three disciples were all fully enlightened beings – *arahants*.

When the Buddha arrived the monks greeted him in the traditional manner. He asked if they were living in harmony and comfort; did they have any problems with almsfood? Venerable Anarudha said, 'We have no problems Lord. Indeed we are well supported and live in harmony.' The Buddha asked, 'How is this so?' Anarudha responded, saying how he considered it a great blessing to have such companions and that he had decided to give up personal preferences; he would do what was conducive to harmony within the community. The Buddha praised Anarudha and asked further, 'Do you live diligently?' Anarudha said, 'Yes Lord, we do.' And the Buddha asked, 'What is it that you do Anarudha?'

Anarudha described briefly ways in which they took care of each other. For example: the first one back from the almswalk set out the mats for sitting upon and would see that the bowls for drinking and washing were in place. And after the meal, the last to finish would put everything away and clean up. They helped each other fill the jars with drinking water and also carry water for the toilets.

Once a week they sat up all night discussing the Dhamma and practising meditation. But the most significant point, and it is emphasized several times in this sutta, is where Anarudha says, 'I dwell with a heart of loving-kindness for my companions, both in public and in private. My mind is attuned to theirs, to the extent that there is only one mind.' The other two bhikkhus when asked, responded in the same way. The Buddha again praised and encouraged them to continue.

It's inspiring to see how perfectly enlightened beings found that the practice of metta or loving-kindness was what brought harmony and peace. It was manifest in the world by their being sensitive to the needs of those they lived with. Even from the perspective of an *arahant*, mundane and obvious gestures of help are very important. These are the things which lead on to concord. I've found reflecting on this quite helpful over the years.

Also in the suttas it mentions 'eleven benefits' from practising metta bhavana. The first benefit is that one falls asleep easily and contented. The second is that one wakes easily, contented and happy. The third is that one is loved by other human beings, and the fourth is that even non-human beings love one. And there is a list of all the harmful and poisonous things from which one is protected. Also it's said that metta bhavana makes the mind easily concentrated, and that the face of one who practises metta is serene and radiant. The tenth benefit is that one dies unconfused. The eleventh benefit states that if one has not penetrated with insight the nature of the mind, then the power of metta bhavana will bring about birth in the heavenly realms.

A very significant thing about this practice for me is the tolerance for oneself that develops. Some of the questions asked on this retreat indicate that people are still being trapped by the same old syndrome, the struggle with not wanting what is. We set up what we like against what we dislike. Thoughts and fantasies become the enemy – that which we feel we have to get rid of and escape from.

How we react in each case depends on the nature of the particular condition. If we perceive it as threatening, then we try to run away from it. When fear arises, for example, we always react with wanting to get away; we want to get some space between us and it. And, of course, as soon as we do that, we empower that condition, we give it life. And it stays with us and disturbs us until we stop reacting.

As a result of what happened to me in Vietnam I have suffered from what they call 'post-trauma syndrome'. They've done tests on Vietnam veterans and found that a lot of them have this particular anxiety reaction as a result of past trauma. Now it's very nice having a label for it, but that doesn't make it go away. I know from years of experience that as long as there is resistance to fear then it has power over us. Metta bhavana is wonderful when dealing with such conditions. We become less adamant about trying to get rid of them. There is a willingness to befriend them and to see that they are just feelings we are experiencing – even the ugly, gruesome, terrifying aspects of the mind.

So, for several days now we have been practising with 'May I be well, may others be well,' and perhaps you have noticed that a feeling of goodwill, of metta, begins to arise. When that feeling happens, we can let go of the thought 'May I be well...' and pay closer attention to those actual feelings. Then we can take it a step further and direct those feelings outwards; *radiate* feelings of goodwill. That word 'outwards' is used quite carefully. One can experience feelings of loving-kindness pervading all directions, filling our world with friendliness, with care, with loving concern. That which was previously troublesome, suddenly in those moments is not. And over a period of time, our attitudes towards ourselves slowly change. There is greater patience and merciful self-forgiveness. In this way, metta bhavana can be used as a skilful means for calming the mind and clearing our attitudes, to provide a suitable base for the practice of *vipassana*, insight meditation.

When I was last in Thailand at Wat Pah Pong, I had a conversation with Ajahn Liam, who is now the abbot there. We were talking about practice, and he mentioned that metta bhavana has certain limitations. One is that we can easily become attached to it, and thereby create an obstacle. There is no question about the benefits of this practice, but sometimes people get really quite high. It can be a very joyful and powerful experience, but that's not liberation. That which brings about insight and understanding is the practice of looking into the mind – investigation, or vipassana.

So for the remainder of this retreat, I want to introduce what might be called the 'wisdom factor'. Having practised metta bhavana for several days, we can begin to *investigate* the mind. The purpose of this practice is to be able to see what is actually happening here and now; to discern the changeability of what is happening, and to see that it is not going to give us the satisfaction we are seeking. Another thing we realize is that all that is happening can be observed. Seeing this is something of enormous importance to us. We see clearly that it is not ours.

The 'skilful means' I would like to introduce tonight, and link with what we have been doing, is to simply ask the question, 'Who?' 'Who is it that is practising metta bhavana? Who is it that is listening now? Who is it that is sitting, who is in pain, who is wondering, who is confused, who is doubting, who is happy, who isn't happy? Who is this?'

Intentionally bring up the question 'Who?' and notice clearly what state of mind follows. The mind stops! We can struggle to find some intellectual answer; maybe our name comes to fill in the gap or maybe an exalted, inspired idea like 'The Original Mind'. But the Original Mind is not the thought 'Original Mind'.

Buddha-nature is not the thought 'Buddha-nature'. Thinking is just thinking. Thought does not really answer the question 'Who?'

Now if we are not careful we could use the question 'Who?' like a club or a sledge-hammer. We could try to pulverize any thoughts that arise in the mind. The questioning needs to be pursued with a sense of inquiry; an almost childlike curiosity. When we see children investigating something new, we see their delight and inquisitiveness. Such an attitude would be wonderful for inquiring into the nature of 'Who?'

In this way we can get another perspective on those things that disturb us. Restlessness, for instance: 'Who is restless?' The answer comes: 'I am.' Who is that? 'Who is walking? Who is sitting?' This practice can cut away very effectively at our thinking, speculating and fantasizing.

I know, however, from personal experience that not everyone can immediately make use of this technique. So don't feel that it is being offered as THE practice. It is a skilful means with particular benefits. It has a simplicity and clarity that I personally like. If you find you can't do it, or it doesn't make any sense, then go back to the practice of metta bhavana. Continue to nurture that sense of goodwill. This will provide a suitable ambiance for the skilful means of asking 'Who?', if or when you choose to use it.

Sometimes asking 'Who?' can become rather dry – even stark and barren – whereas metta bhavana can be very uplifting and inspiring. Hopefully, these two skilful means combined will be a good recipe for insightful practice and lead to understanding and peace.

GUIDED METTA MEDITATION

This meditation could be used in a group, with one person reading the instructions slowly and quietly. A series of dots at the end of a paragraph (. . . .) indicates a brief period of silence before continuing with the next instruction. It is suggested that the meditation take approximately half an hour.

This will be a meditation on loving-kindness. It will incorporate a simple visualization using a faculty of mind that we use quite routinely. For instance, if I suggest bringing to mind the image of a flower, we can do that. It doesn't matter if it's a rose or a lily, or what colour it is, or even how clear that mental image is – something fleeting is adequate.

Now sitting upright, notice if there's any tension in the face. Relaxing around the eyes, around the jaw and mouth. Let the attention come down to the heart area – an area in the middle of the chest, around the sternum, the breastbone. We breathe in, experiencing the breath energy. It's almost as if it's possible to breathe in and out from that area in the middle of the chest. Now as we breathe in, saying to ourselves: MAY I BE WELL – wishing ourselves well, let there be a sense of well-being, a subtle gesture of mercy directed towards ourselves. Let the past be; letting it go: and for this moment in time, just keep letting the mind come to the breath, and the heart, and the thought, in an harmonious whole. Breathing in: MAY I BE WELL . . . and then breathing out, directing that same merciful energy outwards, saying: MAY OTHERS BE WELL.

Continue letting a simple rhythm develop – Breathe in: MAY I BE WELL, breathe out: MAY OTHERS BE WELL. . . . .

If the mind has wandered off, gently, with great patience, bring the attention back. It's a soft movement, coming back to the heart, to the breath, to the thought – breathing in: MAY I BE WELL, breathing out through the heart: MAY OTHERS BE WELL. . . . .

85

What we are doing is beginning to attune ourselves to that which is loving and compassionate in the universe. Opening up to that caring energy and allowing it to energize us, nourish us, using the breath and the thought as a channel, as a vehicle for that energy. Breathing in: MAY I BE WELL. And then channel that energy out to others: MAY OTHERS BE WELL. ....

Keeping the breath soft and steady, letting the breath energy nourish us; breathing in to the heart, breathing out through the heart. ....

Opening up to that which is compassionate in the universe. Breathing in, letting the heart become more sensitive and receptive to that energy. Breathing out, the heart becoming more open and expansive, giving out: MAY OTHERS BE WELL. ....

And when we are ready . . . take a slow, deep breath into the heart, letting the thought and breath energy fill us. Holding it for a while – keeping it comfortable. Allowing the thought to deepen that sense of well-being. Letting it saturate us, permeate the body. Breathing out, slowly, quietly, back out through the heart: MAY OTHERS BE WELL. Doing that a few times – deep breath in, hold it, and out. ....

Now we begin to use the visualization, working more with the out-breath. On the in-breath continue as before, breathing into the heart with the thought: MAY I BE WELL. And on the out-breath, we first bring to mind the image of our parents – it doesn't matter where they are, near or far, alive or dead. Bringing them up one at a time, or together – whichever is easier. Seeing them a few feet in front of us, and each time we breathe out bringing up that image and directing our thoughts of kindness and acceptance towards them. So breathing in with the thought: MAY I BE WELL . . . and breathing out, with the mental image of our parents. As we breathe out: MAY THEY BE WELL. ....

Next: bringing to mind our spiritual teachers, those who have helped us, guided us, encouraged us, instructed us throughout our life. With the out-breath, a gesture of gratitude, using the thought: MAY THEY BE WELL. ....

Bringing to mind now our family; partner, children, brothers and sisters – one at a time, or in a group. With the out-breath, a gesture of affection: MAY THEY BE WELL. Breathing into the heart: MAY I BE WELL, breathing out through the heart: MAY THEY BE WELL. ....

Now bringing to mind a special friend or friends – those whom we feel would benefit from thoughts of kindness. With the out-breath, bringing them into the mind and wishing them well; a subtle embrace, a gesture of caring. ....

Breathing into the heart: MAY I BE WELL. Breathing out through the heart: MAY THEY BE WELL. ....

Bringing to mind now those whom we practise with, those in our immediate environment; directing our thoughts out, including all of them: MAY THEY ALL BE WELL AND AT PEACE. ....

Now bringing to mind an image of the Earth as if seen from outer space. Towards that beautiful blue, white, green, brown image, directing our thoughts: MAY ALL BEINGS BE WELL. Breathing out: MAY ALL BEINGS BE WELL. ....

And now bringing to mind an image of spaciousness, emptiness. Into that vastness directing our thoughts: MAY ALL BEINGS BE WELL. Letting the mind open up, open out; letting the heart open up, open out. The body drops away – no boundaries – vastness – spaciousness. ....

Now carefully, in a slightly more focussed way, bringing our attention back to the heart, a point in the middle of the chest, and breathing in slowly and deeply with the thought: MAY I BE WELL. Holding it for a while.... Letting that thought spread as a sense of well-being throughout the body, energizing and nourishing us. With the out-breath, slowly and quietly, back out through the heart. Doing that once or twice – deep breath in, hold it, and out. ....

Now bringing to mind an image of someone you hurt, intentionally or not, alive or dead... and using their name, saying: PLEASE FORGIVE ME.... Calling to mind someone you hurt... using their name saying: PLEASE FORGIVE ME.

Paying very close attention to the heart. Keeping it open... and now bringing to mind an image of someone who hurt you. Using their name saying: I FORGIVE YOU.... Bringing to mind someone who hurt you. Using their name saying: I FORGIVE YOU.

Now using our own name, we say: I FORGIVE YOU.... Using our own name, we say: I FORGIVE YOU... and ... YOU ARE FORGIVEN... YOU ARE FORGIVEN.

Being *with* those feelings of caring. Bringing them into the heart; holding them gently... Now carefully coming back to the breath – the breath energy coming into the heart with the thought: MAY I BE WELL. Being nourished, filled. And back out, out through the heart for others: MAY OTHERS BE WELL.

So simple – breathing in, being energized. Breathing out, wishing others well. Breathing out for others. ....

Bell to end meditation.

VENERABLE TIRADHAMMO

Venerable Tiradhammo (Ian Adams) was born in New Westminster, British Columbia, in 1949. Whilst reading engineering, geology and geography at the University of British Columbia, he interrupted his studies to undertake a long overland trip in the Middle East, culminating in a cycle ride from Pakistan to Sri Lanka. He stayed for a fortnight at the Island Hermitage in Sri Lanka, and spent a further month practising meditation at Kanduboda Meditation Centre with Bhikkhu Sivoli.

Back in Canada, he completed his university studies, after which he returned to India and later went on to Thailand, where he became a novice in 1973. He took *upasampada* one year later at Wat Meung Man in Chiang Mai with Venerable Tong.

In 1975 he moved, in order to be with Ajahn Chah, staying at Wat Pah Pong and Wat Pah Nanachat. He went on several *tudong* journeys through the north-east of Thailand and the mountains of Chiang Mai, visiting many famous forest meditation masters.

Venerable Tiradhammo was invited to England in 1982 to help with developments there. He spent two years at Chithurst Monastery, and three years in charge of Harnham Vihara in Northumberland. He is presently the senior incumbent of a newly opened vihara near Bern, Switzerland, and is engaged in writing a book on *Vinaya,* the monastic code of conduct.

JOY IN SPIRITUAL PRACTICE

The following teaching has been adapted from a talk given by Venerable Tiradhammo on the seventh day of a ten-day retreat in Switzerland, in May 1988. The 'Seven Factors of Enlightenment' referred to in the talk are mindfulness, investigation, energy, joy, relaxation, concentration and equanimity.

> **When there is joy, we are ready to discover new things.... If we have already decided 'Life is suffering,' then we won't look any further.**

WE CAN SOMETIMES MAKE THE MISTAKE in practice of thinking that the religious life means some sort of self-flagellation. Or, we tend to believe that spiritual practice should result in some *special* kind of purity. With this idea we look at ourselves and, of course, all we see is impurity; having developed a concept of enlightenment, we examine our own minds and see just the opposite – confusion and conflict.

But the point is, these ideas we have about practice are *just* ideas. Thinking: 'I'm here and Nibbana is over there; I'm just a confused idiot and Nibbana is all purity and profundity,' is merely projecting onto concepts. When it comes down to real practice, enlightenment means *actually* being aware of confusion itself. Wisdom is that which is aware of ignorance. It's not a matter of knowing our wisdom, but of *using* wisdom to know ignorance!

The whole practice of mindfulness is about realizing the true nature of this being right here. We're not trying to plug into some kind of 'Nibbanic Wisdom' that's floating around in space or waiting for wisdom to fall into our laps. We are being aware of the nature of the human condition as it is. Once we really understand life as it is, *then* we can begin to transcend it. If we try to transcend it before we actually know it, we're merely caught up in illusion.

Ajahn Chah used to say: 'First we have to pick things up before we can realize how heavy they are.' When we see how heavy they are, then that's *seeing* 'dukkha'. Having seen dukkha, we let go. When we've let go of things then we realize how light it actually is. 'Ah! What a relief.' And this is where joy comes in – or *piti* as it's called in the 'Factors of Enlightenment'.

There are various translations of this term *piti*. As there are various kinds of joy. We were talking yesterday about how, having been motivated by dukkha to seek the 'Way', we arrive at trust – and this trust in turn conditions joy.

So we have these various kinds of joy arising in practice from different causes, and, personally I've found reflecting upon them very useful. The point of joy and its function often seems to be missed when talking about spiritual training.

Now *piti* is not just the pleasure of having a good time. But it's the kind of experience that leads to opening up to life – to awakening. When there is joy, we are ready to discover new things. On the other hand, if we have already decided 'Life is suffering', and judged it as 'miserable', then we won't look any further.

Consider children: notice how they observe and want to find out – the fascination they have about things. Sadly, as adults, we've become too sophisticated to go around looking into flowers and little things. We function on a much more conceptual level. When we see a flower we think 'flower'. And then, 'Yes, I know all about flowers. I've seen flowers all my life and this is just another flower.' Actually, each flower is a unique flower: it is here, at this moment, this time, this place, this flower.

If we can truly listen, for instance, to a bird singing; there is just sound. And that's quite different from thinking, 'Oh, another bird singing.' If we *really* listen, there is simply sound happening right in this moment, in this place, in this situation; and there is a knowing of that – there's hearing. And that's a *completely* different reality from thinking 'bird singing'.

If we are always falling back into concepts, then the internal dialogue goes chattering on: 'Bird singing. Flower over there. This person talking. I wish they'd be quiet. Candle burning...' and so on. *And we think we know all about life!* We continually juggle these concepts around in our heads and all they ever do is move from one side of the brain to the other – out of the memory to be verbalized, then back again. If we live with only concepts of life, it can get pretty boring – it's the same old words – 'flower, bird, tree'.

While it's natural that we learn and understand through language, and express our understanding through language, many of us have become prisoners of language. With meditation we have the opportunity now to bring about a profound change in our Western civilization. We are trying to understand on a 'non-conceptual' level. In meditation we are realizing the nature of experience directly.

People who are completely identified with words may find this threatening, but we're not talking about by-passing words altogether; we still have to express ourselves; we still need to communicate. But we should recognize that the words we use in communication are not the same as the experience we are attempting to convey.

Such little space is given in our society to silence. Words have become so loud and so powerful these days that sometimes that is *all* we hear. But it is the very space of silence that gives us access to, and nurtures, another way of relating. How wonderful to be like a child again and not be limited by words!

In the beginning, children don't have a word for a flower. 'What is this?' they enquire. And we tell them: 'It's a flower.' So okay, they have to learn to communicate, but maybe we should try saying, 'Well, it's *called* a flower, but that's not what it *really* is. It has its own perfect nature which is just-the-way-it-is.' To know this 'just-the-way-it-is' is to know joy. And knowing joy means we can bring back to life many of those beautiful qualities that have become drained out of us. We have a secret key now that will help free us from our habits.

The quality of joy can also be developed further. Beyond *piti* or spiritual joy there is a much more stable quality known as *sukha*. Generally, this term *sukha* is translated merely as happiness – the opposite of *dukkha* – but that's not enough. Momentary happiness is like a butterfly that flitters around. It's certainly O.K., but it's not the profound quality of well-being that is meant by *sukha*. Through having lived so much in concepts, our life has become boring, and fleeting excitement has come to appear as important to us.

Sukha, on the other hand, means: 'Everything is just fine.' It's a sense of calm and well-being which pervades our whole body and mind. It makes the mind peaceful and collected, providing a firm foundation for *samadhi* – concentration.

But coming back to joy: joy is spontaneous. You can't preconceive it. You can't make it. It just arises in the moment. When there is true joy, you are in the moment. And joy in this way becomes a valuable reference point for us: if there is true joy, then we know we're *in* the moment, and if we are really *in* the moment, then there is true joy.

So try to discover where joy comes from. See what supports it and what causes it to pass away. When we are doing this, we are beginning to cultivate joy as one of the 'Factors of Enlightenment'. It becomes one of the qualities that leads us to awakening.

VENERABLE VIRADHAMMO

Venerable Viradhammo (Vitauts Akers) was born at Esslingen in Germany in 1947 to Latvian refugee parents. They moved to Toronto, Canada, when he was 5 years old. He studied engineering at the University of Toronto but became disillusioned with academic life, and left in 1969 to go and work in Germany. Later, while living in India, he encountered Buddhism, meeting the late Samanera Bodhesako, who introduced him to the writings of Venerable Ñanavira Thera. He eventually travelled to Thailand to become a samanera at Wat Mahathat and took *upasampada* in 1974 at Wat Pah Pong. He was one of the first residents at Wat Pah Nanachat.

Having spent four years in Thailand, he went back to Canada and Germany to visit his family in 1977. Instead of returning to Thailand, he was asked by Ajahn Chah to join Ajahn Sumedho at the Hampstead Vihara, in London. In subsequent years, he was involved in the establishment of both Chithurst and Harnham monasteries.

In 1985, on invitation by the Wellington Theravada Buddhist Association, he moved to New Zealand, accompanied by Venerable Thanavaro. At first they lived in the city of Wellington itself, moving two years later to a 43-acre site in Stokes Valley, 29 km away. The monastery was named 'Bodhinyanarama' by Ajahn Sumedho, who conducted the first *upasampada* ceremony there in 1989.

Venerable Viradhammo undertakes a wide range of teaching activities, including monthly visits to a vihara which has been established in Auckland. On occasion he also teaches in the South Island.

SO WHAT

The following teaching on the 'Four Noble Truths' is taken from a talk given by Venerable Viradhammo during a ten-day retreat conducted in Bangkok for Thai lay people, in June 1988.

This teaching is not aimed at just getting another kind of experience. It is about complete freedom within any experience.

THIS EVENING WE MIGHT BEGIN by considering the legend of the life of the Lord Buddha. Now we could consider this story as factual history. Or, we could also look at it as a sort of myth – a story that reflects back on our own development as beings seeking truth.

In the story we are told that before his enlightenment, the Bodhisatta (Buddha-to-be) lived in a royal family with a lot of power and influence. He was a very gifted person, and had all that any human being could wish for: wealth, intelligence, charm, good looks, friendship, respect, and many skills. He lived the princely life of luxury and ease.

The legend has it that when the Bodhisatta was first born, his father the king received a prediction from the wisemen. They said there were two possibilities: either this son would become a world-ruling monarch, or he would become a perfectly enlightened Buddha. Of course the father wanted his son to carry on the business of being a monarch; he didn't want him to become a renunciant. So everybody in the palace was always trying to protect the prince. Whenever anyone grew vaguely old or sick they were taken away; nobody wanted the prince to see anything unpleasant that might cause him to leave.

But then at the age of twenty-nine, curiosity struck. The prince wanted to see what the world outside was like. So off he went out with his charioteer and – what did he see? The first thing he saw was a sick person – all covered with sores, in pain, and lying in his own filth. A thoroughly wretched human condition.

'What's that?' the prince asked his attendant. The attendant replied: 'That's a sick person.' After a discussion the prince realized, for the first time, that these human bodies can become sick and painful. The attendant pointed out that all bodies had this potential. This came as a great shock to the prince.

The following day he went out again. This time he saw an old person: all bent over with age, shaking, wrinkled, grey-haired, barely able to hold himself up. Again, shocked by what he saw, the prince asked: 'What's that?' 'That's an old person,' the attendant replied. 'Everybody grows old.' So the prince realized that his body too had this potential to become old. With that he went back to the palace quite bewildered by it all.

The third time he went out, and saw a dead person. Most of the townsfolk were busy, happily waving at their attractive prince, thinking he was having a great time. But behind the crowds, there were people carrying a stretcher with a corpse on it, going to the funeral pyre. That was a really powerful one for him. 'And *what* is *that*?!' he asked. So the attendant replied: 'That's a corpse. All bodies go that way; your body, my body, they all die.' That really shocked him.

The next time the Bodhisatta went out he saw a mendicant monk – sitting under a tree meditating. 'And who is that?' he asked. The attendant replied: 'That's a *sadhu* – someone who is seeking the answers to life and death.'

So we have this legend. Now what does this mean for you and me? Is it just a historical tale to tell our children, a tale about a person who didn't see old age, sickness or death until he was twenty-nine?

For me, this story represents the awakening of a human mind to the limitations of sensory experience. Personally I can relate to this from a time when I was at university. I questioned life a lot: 'What is it all about?' 'Where is this all going to?' I used to wonder about death, and started thinking: 'What is the point of getting this university degree? Even if I become a famous engineer, or if I become rich, I'm still going to die. If I become the best politician, or the best lawyer, or the best whatever. . . Even if I was to

become the most famous rock star that ever existed... Big deal.'
At that time, I think Jimi Hendrix had just taken too much heroin
and died.

Nothing I thought of could answer the question of death. There
was always: 'So what?... So if I have a family? So if I am famous?
So if I'm not famous? So if I have a lot of money? So if I don't
have a lot of money?' None of these things resolved this doubt:
'What about death? What is it? Why am I here? Why seek any
kind of experience if it all goes to death anyway?'

Questioning all the time like this made it impossible for me to
study. So I started to travel. I managed to distract the mind for
a time, because travelling was interesting: Morocco, Turkey,
India... But I kept coming back to this same conclusion: 'So
what? So if I see another temple, if I see another mosque, if
I eat yet another kind of food – so what?'

Sometimes this doubt arises for people when somebody they know
dies, or if they become sick, or old. It can also come from religious
insight. Something in the mind clicks, and we are awakened to
the fact that no matter what experiences we have, they all
change, they come to an end, they die. Even if I'm the most
famous, powerful, richest, influential person in the world, all that
is going to die. It's going to cease. So this question 'So what?' is an
awakening of the mind.

If we were to do this ten-day retreat with the idea of getting 'a
meditation experience', then 'So what?' We still have to go back
to work, still have to face the world, still have to go back to
Melbourne, still have to go back to New Zealand.... So what!
What is the difference between 'a meditation experience' and
doing a cruise on The Queen Elizabeth II? A bit cheaper maybe!

The Buddhist teaching is not aimed at just getting another kind of
experience. It is about understanding the nature of experience
itself. It is aimed at actually observing what it means to be a
human being. We are contemplating life, letting go of delusion,
letting go of the source of human suffering and realizing truth,
realizing Dhamma. And that's a different process altogether.

When we're doing 'mindfulness of breathing' – *anapanasati* – we're not doing it with the effort to get something later. We're doing it to simply *be* with what is: just *being* with an in-breath, *being* with an out-breath. And what is the result when we're *being* mindful in this way? Well, I think we can all see. The mind becomes calm, our attention is steady – we are aware and *with* the way things are.

So already we are able to see that calming the mind is a healthy and compassionate thing to do for ourselves. Also, notice how this practice creates space in the mind. We can see now the potential for really 'being attentive' to life. Our attention is not caught up. We're not being 'kidnapped' all the time. We can really work with attention.

If we're obsessed with something, then our attention is absorbed into the object of obsession. When we're worried, exhausted, upset, excited, desiring, depressed and so on, our attention energy is lost. So by calming the mind we're creating space and 'freeing' attention.

And there is a beauty in that. When we go outside after this meditation period, maybe we'll notice things in a different way – the green trees, the smells, what we're walking on, the little lotuses in bloom. These pleasant experiences calm and relax us and are very helpful – the same as going on a cruise. In New Zealand they go trekking in the mountains for relaxation.

But this kind of happiness, or *sukha,* is not the full potential of the Buddha. A lot of joy can come with this level of practice, but that is not enough. The happiness of a relatively calm mind is not complete freedom. This is still just another experience. It's still caught in 'So what!'

The complete freedom of the Buddha comes from the work of investigation – *dhammavicaya.* It is completely putting an end to all conflict and tension. No matter where we are in life, there are no more problems. It's called 'the unshakable deliverance of the heart' – complete freedom within any experience.

One of the wonderful things about this Way is that it can be applied in all situations. We don't have to be in a monastery, or even to have a happy feeling, to contemplate Dhamma. We can contemplate Dhamma within misery. We often find that it is when people are suffering that they start coming to the monastery. When they're happy and successful it probably wouldn't occur to them. But if their partner leaves home, or they lose their job, get cancer, or something, then they say, 'Oh, what do I do now?'

So for many of us, the Buddha's teaching begins with the experience of suffering – *dukkha.* This is what we start contemplating. Later on we find that we also need to contemplate happiness – *sukha.* But people don't begin by going to the Ajahn, saying: 'Oh Venerable Sir, I'm so happy! Help me out of this happiness.'

Usually we begin when life says: 'This hurts.' Maybe it's just boredom; for me it was the contemplation of death – this 'So what?' Maybe it's alienation at work. In the West we have what's called 'the middle-age crisis'. Men around the age of forty-five or fifty start to think: 'I've got it all,' or, 'I haven't got it all, so what?' 'Big deal.' Something awakens and we begin to question life. And since everybody experiences dukkha, in its gross and refined aspects, it's beautiful that the Teaching begins here – the Buddha says, 'There is dukkha.' No one can deny that. This is what the Buddhist teaching is based upon – actually observing these experiences we have – observing life.

Now the worldly way of operating with dukkha is to try to get rid of it. Often we use our intelligence to try and maximize sukha and minimize dukkha. We are always trying to figure out how to make things more convenient. I remember a discourse that Luang Por once gave about this.

In the monastery we used to all join in hauling water from the well. There would be two cans of water on a long bamboo pole, and a bhikkhu at each end to carry them. So Ajahn Chah said: 'Why do you always carry water with the monk that you like? You should carry water with the monk you dislike!' This was true. I was a very speedy novice and would always try to avoid carrying water with a slow old bhikkhu in front. It drove me crazy. Sometimes I'd get stuck behind one of them, and be pushing away...

So having to carry water with a monk I disliked was dukkha. And, as Ajahn Chah said, I would always try to figure out how to have things the way I wanted. That's using intelligence to try to maximize sukha and minimize dukkha. But of course even if we do get what we want, we still have dukkha; because the pleasure of gratification is not permanent – it is *anicca*. Imagine eating something really delicious; in the beginning it would feel pleasurable. But if you had to eat that for four hours! It would be awful.

So what do we do with dukkha? The Buddhist teaching says: use intelligence to really look at it. That's why we put ourselves in a retreat situation like this with the Eight Precepts. We're actually looking at dukkha rather than just trying to maximize sukha. Monastic life is based on this also; we're trapped in these robes. But then we have an incredible freedom to look at suffering – rather than just ignorantly trying to get rid of it.

Wearing these robes in the West can be really difficult. It's not like wearing a robe in Thailand! When we first moved to London I felt so out of place. As a lay person I always dressed to not be noticed, but in that situation we were up front all the time. That was dukkha for me; I felt very self-conscious. People were looking at me all the time. Now, if I had had the freedom to maximize sukha and minimize dukkha, I would have put on a pair of jeans, a brown shirt, grown a beard and been one of the mob. But I couldn't do that because I had renunciation precepts. Renunciation is giving up the tendency to always try to maximize pleasure. I really learned a lot in that situation.

We all have responsibilities: family, job, career and so on. And these are kinds of limitations, aren't they? What do we do with them? Rather than resent these limitations and say: 'Oh if only it were different, I would be happy,' we can consider: 'Now this is a chance to understand.' We say: 'This is the way it is now. There is dukkha.' We actually go towards that dukkha; we make it conscious – bring it into mind. We don't have to create dukkha especially, there's already enough suffering in this world. But the encouragement of the teachings is to actually *feel* the dukkha that we have in life.

Maybe on this retreat you find during a sitting that you are bored and restless, and waiting for the bell to ring. Now you can actually notice that. If we didn't have this form, then we could just walk out. But what happens if I walk out on restlessness? I might think I've gotten rid of restlessness, but have I? I go and watch T.V. or read something – I keep that restlessness going. And then I find my mind is not peaceful: it's filled with activity. Why? Because I've followed sukha and tried to get rid of dukkha. That is the constant, painful, restlessness of our lives. It is so unsatisfactory, so unpeaceful – not Nibbana.

The First Noble Truth of the Buddhist teaching is not saying, 'Get this experience.' It says look at the experience of dukkha. We are not expected to merely believe in Buddhism as a 'teaching', but to look at dukkha – without judging. We are not saying I shouldn't have dukkha. Nor are we just thinking about it. We're actually feeling it – observing it. We're bringing it to mind. So, there is dukkha.

The teaching then goes on to consider that dukkha has a cause and also that it has an end. A lot of Westerners think that Buddhism is a very negative teaching, because it talks about suffering. When I first had the inspiration to become a Buddhist monk, I was in India. Then my grandfather died so I went back to Germany for the funeral. I tried to talk to my mother about ordination. But when I mentioned suffering, she got quite upset; she took it quite personally. She didn't understand what I was saying: that this is simply what human beings have to go through.

So the Buddha wasn't just talking about dukkha. He was also talking about the cause of dukkha, the end of dukkha and a path to that end. This teaching is about enlightenment – *Nibbana.* And that is what this Buddha-image is saying. It's not an image of the Buddha suffering. It's of his enlightenment; it's all about freedom.

But to be enlightened we have to take what we've got, rather than try to get what we want. In the worldly way we usually try to *get* what we want. All of us want Nibbana – right? – even though we don't know what it is. When we're hungry, we go to the fridge and get something, or we go to the market and get something. Getting, getting, always getting something. . . . But if we try to *get* enlightenment like that, it doesn't work. If we could get enlightenment the same way as we get money, or get a car, it would be rather easy. But it's more subtle than that. It takes intelligence – *pañña*. It takes investigation, *dhammavicaya*.

So now we're using intelligence not to maximize sukha and minimize dukkha, but to actually look at dukkha. We're using intelligence to consider things skilfully. 'Why am I suffering?' So you see, we're not dismissing thought, thought is a very important faculty. But if we can't think clearly then it's not really possible to use the Buddhist teachings. However, you don't need a Ph.D. in Buddhism either.

Once when I was in England, we went to go see a chap in Lancaster. He had just finished a 'Master's' thesis on *sunyata* – ten thousand words on emptiness. He wanted to make us a cup of coffee. So he put the coffee in the cups with the sugar and milk, and offered them to us – forgetting to put in the water. He could do a 'Master's' degree on emptiness, but it was more difficult to mindfully make a cup of coffee. So intelligence in Buddhism isn't just an accumulation of ideas. It's more grounded than that. It's grounded in experience.

Intelligence is the ability to observe life and to ask the right questions. We're using thought to direct the mind in the right way. We're observing and opening the mind to the situation. And it is in this openness, with the right questions, that we have *vipassana* practice: insight into the way we are. The mind is taking the concepts of the teaching, and channeling intelligence towards human experience. We're opening, being attentive, and realizing the way things are. This investigation of the Four Noble Truths is the classic application of intelligence in Theravada Buddhism.

So simply observing dukkha is not trying to get an experience, is it? It is accepting responsibility for our dukkha – our inner conflict. We *feel* the inner conflict – 'I am suffering.' And we ask: 'What is the cause?'

The teaching says, dukkha begins and ends – it's not permanent. Suppose I'm feeling uncomfortable during the sitting, and I turn to that dukkha and ask: 'What is the cause of this suffering?' 'It's because the body is uncomfortable,' comes the answer. So I decide to move. But after five minutes, I find the body is uncomfortable again. So this time, I look at the feeling a little more closely. And I notice something more: 'I *don't want* discomfort. I *want* pleasant feeling.' Ah! So it's not the painful feeling that's the problem – it's the *not wanting* the painful feeling. Now that is a very useful insight, isn't it? That's a bit deeper. I find that now I can be at peace with painful feeling and don't *have* to move. I don't get restless and the mind becomes quite calm.

So I've seen that the cause of the problem isn't the painful feeling – it's the 'not wanting' that particular feeling. 'Wanting' is quite tricky stuff. It comes in many forms. But we can always apply this same investigation: 'What is it I want now?' The Second Noble Truth – *samudaya* – says that the cause of suffering is attachment to wanting – *tanha*. It makes us feel that if we get what we want we'll be fulfilled: 'If I have this' or 'If I become that' or 'If I get rid of this and don't have that'. . . . And that's *samsara* rolling on. Desire and fear, pushing beings into always becoming: always seeking rebirth, leading endless busy lives.

But the Buddha says that there is also 'a way out'. There is an end to suffering. The end of suffering we call *nirodha* – cessation – or *Nibbana*. When I first read about Nibbana, I understood it to mean no greed, no hatred and no delusion. So I thought if only I can get rid of all greed, hatred and delusion, then that would be Nibbana – it seemed that way. I tried and it didn't work. I got more confused.

But as I continued to practise, I found that the 'cessation of suffering' meant the ending of these things in their own time – they have their own energy. I couldn't say to myself: 'O.K. Tomorrow I'm not going to be greedy or afraid.' That was a ridiculous idea. What we have to do is to 'contain' these energies until they die – until they cease. If I felt angry and were to act on it, maybe I would kick someone in the shins. Then they'd kick me back, and we'd have a fight. Or, I'd go back to my hut and meditate, and hate myself. It goes on and on because I've reacted to it. If I'm either following it or trying to get rid of it, then it doesn't cease. The fire doesn't die.

The Teaching of the Four Noble Truths says then: we have suffering – *dukkha*; there is a cause – *samudaya*; there is an end – *nirodha*; and a path to that end – *magga*. This is such a practical teaching. In any situation of inner conflict we can take responsibility for what we're feeling: 'Why am I suffering? What am I wanting now?' We can investigate – using *dhammavicaya*.

It is important that we actually apply these Teachings. Luang Por used to say: 'Sometimes people who are very close to Buddhism are like ants that crawl around on the outside of the mango. They never actually taste the juice.' Sometimes we hear the structure of the teachings and think we understand – 'It's just a way of observing life,' we say. But the teachings are not just an intellectual structure. They are saying that experience itself has a structure which must be understood.

So we're not merely using intelligence to maximize sukha and minimize dukkha. We are using it to free the mind, to go beyond, to realize the unshakable deliverance of the heart, to realize Nibbana. We're using intelligence for freedom, not just frivolity; to liberate the mind, not just to be happy. We're going beyond happiness and unhappiness. We're not just trying to get another experience – it is a different attitude altogether.

I'll leave you with that for tonight.

VENERABLE BRAHMAVAMSO

Venerable Brahmavaṁso (Peter Betts) was born in London in 1951. His first contact with Buddhism came while browsing in a bookshop in London while still at school. He went to Cambridge University to study physics, during which time he became a member of the local Buddhist society and started to practise meditation. After graduating with First Class Honours, he taught physics for a while at a secondary school in Devon. However, his contact with Thai bhikkhus in London inspired him to go to Thailand to take up the bhikkhu life himself, and he received bhikkhu ordination at Wat Sraket at the age of 23, with Tan Chao Khun Prom Gunaphorn.

From 1975, he trained under Ajahn Chah, being one of the first residents at Wat Pah Nanachat. In 1983 he joined Venerable Jagaro at the newly established Bodhinyana Monastery in Perth, Western Australia, where he still lives. He has been actively involved in the major building programme, and teaches Buddhism to a wide and varied audience, ranging from children to local prisoners.

Venerable Brahmavaṁso is known amongst the community of Western monks for his erudition in the *Vinaya*, the monastic code of conduct, and his work in this area currently provides the foundation for *Vinaya* instruction to Westerners in the monasteries in England, Switzerland, Australia and New Zealand.

BECOMING ENLIGHTENED

**So there I was, in a foreign land, trying so hard,
giving up so much – and for what?
I wasn't quite sure.**

WHEN I WAS VERY YOUNG I WANTED DESPERATELY to
become a train driver. My grandfather had taken my brother and
me to Euston Station in London where I began an infatuation
with those massive, black and green steel machines that hissed,
with so much strength. Wouldn't it be wonderful, I dreamt,
one day . . . if . . .

Some years later I wanted desperately to become enlightened. I
had read all about it in the books. To a starry-eyed young man, the
idea of living in permanent bliss and saving humanity at the same
time was irresistibly appealing. Wouldn't it be wonderful, I used to
dream, one day . . . if . . .

When I first heard the story of the Lord Buddha's enlightenment,
I was still many glasses of beer away from being a monk. I was a
student, doing most of those outrageous activities students
enjoyed in the late sixties – and regretted in the late seventies. But
I had been meditating off and on – mostly the former – for some
time, and I had begun to notice some unmistakable changes in my
daily life. I was attending the Vesak celebration at the local
Buddhist Society and as the Venerable Sri Lankan monk was
reading out the Enlightenment Story, I became more and more
inspired and excited. I especially relished the bit where the
Buddha-to-be sat at the root of the Bodhi Tree and made that
earth-shaking resolution:

> 'Though my blood dries up and my bones turn to dust, I will
> not move from this spot until I have penetrated to Supreme
> and Complete Enlightenment!'

Wow! As the story moved on, a thought began to solidify in
my mind. I could hardly wait until the end of the chanting. I

impatiently gulped down the cup of tea which was all but obligatory at the occasion, and then I hurried back to my room at college. I had heard enough talks on Buddhism, I had read plenty of books on the subject. I had been meditating for a whole year now, at least once a week – well most weeks anyway. If the Buddha could do it, why not me?

Thus it was that I, in the arrogant stupidity of youth, a novice meditator who could hardly manage to sit still for thirty minutes, decided that it was time to become enlightened. It was now or never, I resolved, for the next day I had an exam. I locked the door of my room. I sat down on my meditation cushion. I collected myself. Then I pronounced in a low, clear, solemn voice:

> 'Though my blood dries up and my bones turn to dust,
> I will not move from this very cushion until I, also,
> become enlightened.'

That was it. No more mucking about. I was dead serious.

Forty minutes later I was in extreme agony. Though my blood appeared as liquid as ever and no disintegration of my bones was discernible yet, my knees were giving me hell! What was really worrying me though, was that over half an hour had gone by and I hadn't seen the anticipated brilliant and flashing lights yet. There hadn't even been a twinkle to suggest that I was getting near. It was very depressing – and very painful. I gave in. I got up very disappointed. Not becoming enlightened had spoiled the whole day.

A few years later and a little more sensible – though only a little – I was at London airport being sent off to Thailand by two Thai bhikkhus. I was going to Bangkok to be ordained. I still remember the parting words of the senior of the bhikkhus, who was my teacher then: 'Please come back when you become enlightened.' I was planning to be a monk in Thailand for two years at most. I had told my relatives and friends that I'd be back within two summers. After all, two whole years as a Buddhist monk in Thailand – surely that is long enough even for those of slow intelligence to become enlightened. As for me, I had a degree from university, so there was no doubt in my mind that I would be back in England within two years, enlightened. Once I had got that out of the way, I planned to get married and go live in a commune – in Wales of course. I had made enquiries before I left.

Two years down the track, it was becoming obvious that this enlightenment business might not be so easy. For some reason, though I was a Westerner with a good degree from a top university, I was acting more stupidly than the Thai monks who had barely finished grade four in village schools. My conceit was taking a fair hammering. The strange thing was that, even though I still wasn't enlightened, I was enjoying the peace, simplicity and morality of monastic life. I didn't want to leave. What I had in mind to do on the commune in Wales had lost its appeal.

In my fourth Rains Retreat I was pulling out all the stops. Word had come to Thailand that Chithurst House had been bought, a Sangha was being established in England and they needed more bhikkhus. This would be a great time to become enlightened. I was in a very quiet monastery. My meditation practice was in high gear. All the omens were favourable. Then it happened!

Walking on my meditation path one evening, my mind already calm from many hours of sitting, I suddenly understood the cause of all problems and my heart immediately felt the joy of release. All around seemed brilliant. Bliss filled my whole being. Energy and clarity were there in abundance. Though it was late at night I sat in meditation perfectly mindful, perfectly still. Then I lay down to rest, sleeping oh-so-lightly for just a few hours. I rose at 3 a.m. and was first in the grass Meeting Hall for the morning meditation. I sat through until dawn as if without effort and without the slightest drowsiness. That was it! It was immeasurable joy being enlightened. Pity it didn't last long.

The monastery where this happened was very poor and the food was very coarse. It was the sort of North-Eastern Thai monastery where you were happy to eat just one meal a day – facing such an ordeal twice in one day being beyond the pale! The morning after my experience of 'release', though, the fare was more reasonable. Along with the staple 'rotten-fish curry', which is actually made from stewing small fish which have been kept most unhygienically until they go 'off', there was a saucepan of pork curry. That day even the Thai abbot visibly reacted at the sight of the reeking fish stew and took a whopping big helping from the pot of pork curry. I didn't mind; I was second in line and there was plenty left for me. However, the pot of pork never reached me. Instead, the abbot poured what was left of the pork curry into the mess of rotten fish stew and stirred it all up saying that it all gets mixed up in the stomach anyway. I was incensed! Of all the hypocrites! If he really thought that, then why didn't he mix the curries before he took out his share? I peered angrily into the saucepan he handed me – rotten smelly pieces of rubbery fish swimming alongside my delicious pork – my one lucky meal ruined. Oooh, that abbot, was I mad at him! Was I angry!

Then a thought struck me with a depressing thud, or rather a sickening squelch – maybe I wasn't enlightened at all. Enlightened beings aren't supposed to get angry. Arahants don't care if they eat putrid fish or delicious pork. I had to admit I was angry – therefore I had to own up that I wasn't enlightened. What a let-down. Utterly depressed, I scooped a ladle of rotten fish cum pork into my bowl. I was too disappointed to notice the taste of what I ate that day.

In spite of these spiritual hiccups coming from Dhamma-indigestion (a poor ability to assimilate the Teachings), my following years as a bhikkhu were definitely producing results of more tranquillity, clarity and joy. It was the humble insights, the sort which arrive without a fanfare, which were proving the more effective. My wish to become enlightened now appeared suspiciously akin to my childish wish to become a train driver, or to my later ambitions to become the first English astronaut . . . a professional footballer . . : a lead guitarist in a rock band . . . the greatest lover in my college . . . (I am too embarrassed to mention my other aspirations). In a way, wanting to become enlightened was even more foolish. At least I had some idea of what driving a train was about. As for enlightenment, I wasn't quite sure what that was! And whenever I would try to find out by asking one of the senior monks, I would never get a straight answer. So there I was in a very foreign land, eating rotten fish and things much worse, enduring ravenous mosquitoes and unending heat, trying so hard and giving up so much – and for what? I wasn't quite sure. So the only rational thing to do was to give up trying to become enlightened until I knew what enlightenment was! I didn't want to give up being a bhikkhu, I understood that and it made sense. I just had to let go of chasing my fantasies, and my idea of enlightenment was the ultimate fantasy.

On the other side of insight one seldom thinks that one is now wise, for one is overwhelmed by the thought of how stupid one has been. How could I have been so thick? It is written in so many of the Buddhist scriptures, and it is emphasized by so many fine teachers, that BECOMING IS SUFFERING – becoming *anything*. The Buddha, speaking as plain as ever, thundered that he didn't recommend ANY becoming. Becoming is what the ego does all day. Becoming fashions the identity. Becoming is the 'skin' which holds together the bubble of self. Stop all becoming and the illusion is shattered.

So that was the end of my becoming enlightened. I focused instead on the question of WHO it was who wanted to become enlightened, if there was anyone there at all? I investigated no-self, which is much more illuminating than trying to become enlightened. But still people ask me, as they do of other bhikkhus, the bottom-line question: Are you enlightened? Now I have a splendid answer, which I plagiarize from the late Venerable Ananda Mangala Mahanayakathera (I know he won't mind) who, terrific teacher that he was, gave the perfect reply to this very question:

> 'No sir!', replied the venerable Sri Lankan thera, 'I am not enlightened. But I am highly eliminated!'

VENERABLE GAVESAKO

Venerable Gavesako (Mitsuo Shibahashi) was born in Japan in 1951.
An experienced mountaineer, he formed part of a team planning to
climb in the Himalayas. Having arrived in India before the rest of his
party in order to acclimatize, he decided to stay at an Indian ashram.
By the time the party arrived, his interest in meditation had eclipsed
his former interest in climbing, and he decided to stay on at the
ashram, spending two years there in all. As it turned out, the climbing
party met with disaster when some of its members were killed in an
avalanche.

Eventually visa difficulties forced him to move to Thailand, where
he hoped to continue to develop his meditation practice. Having met
Western monks in Bangkok he went up to Wat Pah Pong and was
ordained as a bhikkhu by Ajahn Chah in 1975. He has done many
periods of *tudong* practice, and has spent long periods looking after
Ajahn Chah in the later years of his illness.

In 1989 he was invited back to Japan to spend several months
teaching meditation.

TALKING ABOUT SUFFERING

This is a collection of notes taken during periods of reflection on working with suffering. They were collected by a lay disciple from Bangkok who was visiting Venerable Gavesako.

**We see how desire and attachment are Mara...
and when we are no longer deceived by these
things, then that is the Buddha.**

Taking suffering as our teacher.

DON'T DESPISE SUFFERING; DON'T RUN AWAY FROM IT or be afraid. Suffering warns us not to be complacent. Be wise. Know and see things as they really are; see the truth. If we can bear with it, then the more suffering the better. This way we won't have to be afraid of anything, but we must be patient and persistent. We must be daring. Wherever there is suffering, observe it closely. Suffering needs to be recognized. We must study it and look into it. If we observe like this we will become aware of desire – *tanha* – and attachment – *upadana*. Desire and attachment are what cause suffering, and this same desire and attachment blind us to suffering. We suffer but we don't see suffering. So we must make our minds resolute, go right inward in order to see suffering. When we see it we will know it clearly. There will arise *ñana-dassana*, knowledge and vision according to reality; knowledge that it is only suffering that arises, only suffering that exists, and only suffering that ceases. Other than suffering, nothing arises and nothing ceases.

Sabbe dhamma nalam abhinivesaya: all things are not worthy of clinging to. *Sabbe dhamma anatta*: all things are not-self.

Whatever arises must in time cease. If we can leave things be, let suffering go, neither delighting nor despising, there will be no suffering; or if there is, it will be just as if there isn't.

Depression is a guest.

This feeling of depression has just come for a visit; soon it will leave. Having gone it will come again. If we don't attach to it, it won't stay. So we don't delight in following our moods. When guests come, if we drive them away they'll become angry; but we mustn't be too welcoming either, or they will settle down to stay! Just let them be and they will leave of their own accord. They're only visitors, they are not residents. If they come, we know thus: 'Oh, they've come.' We note it and then leave them be. We establish our mind in equanimity. Centre your mind, not delighting, not despising, not being frightened; neither taking nor rejecting, just keep knowing. The goal is non-suffering: a mind that is calm, clean and clear.

Have you ever experienced so much suffering that you wanted to die?

If we're suffering or depressed, we simply know that suffering or depression exists. It's not necessary for thoughts to proliferate on it. We are patient and observe those feelings – not taking delight in them, and not rejecting them either. Holding our mind still, not letting it lean to the right or to the left. Centring our mind. Just knowing. Sitting, just know; walking, just know. If we keep observing we will begin to understand more clearly. We will see that these things in themselves are empty. We will see that both suffering and depression are merely sensations; they are not our self nor do they belong to us. It is only clinging: clinging to the idea that one is depressed, to the idea that one is suffering. Actually those things can change, and they *will* change of themselves when new sensations arise. They are all *aniccaṁ, dukkhaṁ, anatta* – uncertain, unsatisfactory and not-self.

We suffer because we cling.

We experience suffering and depression only because of clinging and attachment. We must lift our minds to do the work of enquiry using patience and forbearance. If we closely observe the impermanent nature of these feelings, in due course we will see they *do* change. When we see this, we will know what is meant by *sabbe dhamma anatta* – all things are not-self. Then we will see clearly.

Don't think that it's you that is suffering.

Suffering is not *you*; *you* are not suffering. Suffering doesn't abide within *you,* and *you* do not abide in suffering. Suffering arises, exists and ceases. We have the task of simply knowing that suffering arises, knowing that suffering exists, and knowing that suffering ceases. Regardless of however much suffering there may be, if we can observe in this way we will be able to bear with it; we *must* endure. A wise person can endure suffering.

Dhamma is taking things 50%.

If we have thoughts like: 'That person is wrong; they shouldn't have done such a thing'; remember first that *we* may also be wrong; they may not be wrong at all. Take it only 50%. Considering like this we won't allow our thoughts to cause us to suffer.

If someone tells us: 'They've been saying horrible things about you,' or 'Such and such a person is really awful,' don't believe it 100% – but don't reject it either. Take it only 50%. Don't get caught in reacting and feeling unhappy. They may not have actually said such things; the person relating the stories may just be giving their own version. Don't act on other people's thoughts. Often we become angry and upset for no reason other than our own thinking. Be mindful and consider carefully before taking action.

If you are doing something for your partner and at the same time thinking: 'This is totally unreasonable. Why did they ask me to do such a thing. . . ?', this is not right. Don't react like that. Don't hold onto such feelings just because it *appears* unreasonable. They may not have meant what you thought they meant. Thoughts are all *aniccaṁ* – uncertain; they change. Your partner may change their mind; they may have misinterpreted their own thoughts or have not meant what they said. Don't allow these feelings to confuse you. If we are mindful, we won't suffer. Don't believe anything 100%; not ourself, not another, not any condition. Don't be upset or frightened. Don't be surprised at anything you hear or see. Remember: everything is uncertain; only take it 50%.

If you are still suffering, you must look even closer.

Contemplate the Four Noble Truths regularly. If we are still suffering it means we still don't have Right View. When suffering arises, we look inward, not outwards and we don't blame others. We just look at our own body and mind. Look and see how desire and attachment are the cause of suffering. They are *Mara*; our most bitter enemies. Tackle those thoughts with persistence. Know those thoughts. When we know them for what they are, we will be untroubled. We won't become upset. We will no longer be deceived by these things and won't cling to them. Instead, there will be established the One Who Knows, the Awakened One, the Radiant One. There! That's the Buddha. You don't have to search elsewhere. Even if you have to pay for this with your life, it's worth it.

We must have Right Thought and Right View.

Whatever we are doing, we must have mindfulness, clear comprehension, and satisfaction. If we are sweeping the floor, the act of sweeping the floor is the most important thing in the world; anything else is of no importance. When we are sweeping the floor, we *know* we are sweeping the floor – we are mindful of the act of sweeping the floor. We must do it with total satisfaction.

If we are squeezing the juice from oranges, the act of squeezing the juice from oranges is the most important thing in the world; anything else is of no importance. When we are squeezing the juice of oranges, we *know* that we are squeezing the juice of oranges. We are mindful of the act of squeezing the juice of oranges. We must do it with total satisfaction.

Whatever it is that we are doing, sweeping the floor, squeezing juice, cleaning the bathroom; this is our practice. We must not think that we do what we do just to please others. Do not think that we *have* to do it. Do not be worried by what other people might think. We do that which it is our duty to do. And we always do our best. If we look at things this way, if we think in this way, then we won't suffer. We will know peace. We will have great happiness *all* the time. This is Right Thought and Right View.

VENERABLE SUCITTO

Venerable Sucitto was born in London in 1949, but moved to the small town of Dunstable in his teens. His first encounter with Buddhism came through an interest in Japanese literature while at grammar school, but he found nothing to follow it up in his local town. The continuing interest in literature carried him through a B.A. in English and American Literature at Warwick University in 1971. After that, the search for a meaningful direction in life eventually attracted him to take an overland trip through the East, heading for Australia. Following a period in India, he went to Thailand in 1975, where he happened across a class in Buddhist meditation in Chiang Mai. After a few days' practice, he decided to make a tentative commitment to the Holy Life.

He spent three years in Thailand, mostly at Wat Kiriwong in Nakhon Sawan. During a short sojourn in Chiang Mai, however, he met Ajahn Sumedho, before the latter left for England. When Venerable Sucitto himself returned to England in 1978 to visit his family, he met Ajahn Sumedho again at the Hampstead Vihara, and decided to stay and train with him. During the past ten years he has lived for the most part with Ajahn Sumedho, and has been responsible for editing and publishing his talks, as well as other Sangha publications.

Venerable Sucitto was the first senior incumbent of the Harnham Vihara. Since 1983 he has been involved with establishing a training for ten-precept nuns, and in 1984 he moved to Amaravati Buddhist Centre where he still resides.

Kwan Yin and the Noble Elephant

In the winter of 1986-87, Venerable Sucitto was in Thailand; during that time he went wandering (tudong) with Venerable Gavesako. Most of the time was spent in the Isan – the provinces of North-East Thailand – but in the following piece, he reflects on another part of the trip, in Siraja and Ko Sichang. . . .

Something in me let go and listened to the sounds of the world...and the silence behind it all seemed to encompass everything. No sound could stain the silence of the listening mind.

SIRAJA IS NOT A PARTICULARLY BEAUTIFUL TOWN. It's part of that urban overspill to the east of Bangkok that flows along the coast through Samut Pakhan and down to Chonburi, oozing along in the wake of the oil and shipping developments around the Gulf of Thailand. Ajahn Gavesako and I had decided to go there as part of our *tudong* trip, in order to get out to an island called Ko Sichang – The Island of the Noble Elephant. This would be around Christmas time, which like most festive occasions in Thailand is very noisy, at least in the more Western-influenced cities. Accordingly, we planned to stay a night or two at a small monastery that Ajahn Gavesako knew, and then go out to the island for a few days of living very simply, away from the hustle and bustle.

It seemed like a good idea: even before the festival began, life in the city was noisy compared with the forests of the Isan. The little monastery that we were staying in occupied a few acres squashed up against a hillside on the outskirts of the city of Siraja; it wasn't exactly in the heart of town, but it certainly wasn't outside of it. There was a lot of noise from the streets and from Christmas music being played very loudly; so after the initial pleasantries with the resident monks, I for one was quite eager to get away. But of course one has to wait until someone gets to know of one's wishes and offers to buy a ticket – which may take a few days.

So one evening we went down to the seafront and walked out to a small island that was connected the mainland by a pier. On this island there was one of those Chinese Buddhist temples, of which there are very many in Thailand, which go in for the more ritualistic side of Buddhism. In order to obtain good fortune one can make offerings at shrines in such temples – to the Buddha or to one of the bodhisattvas, particularly to the Bodhisattva of Compassion, The One Who Listens to The Sounds Of The World – or Kwan Yin, as she is known in Chinese. I must admit this supplication to divine agencies has never fitted in with my ideas about Buddhism; my mind kept turning away from the painted images and the decorative shrines to the sea, bathed in sunset gold. The serene horizon hinted of sublime planes, and I found myself more eager than ever to get out to a place where I could apply myself whole-heartedly to meditation.

By the next afternoon, unseen wheels had turned and we were able to get a ferry boat out to the island of Ko Sichang. We landed at a little harbour and walked along the coast of the island until we came to a more remote area. There we found a fantastic old ruined temple that had been built in the reign of King Mongkut. It wasn't like the Chinese temple. Its very decay gave it a certain air of sanctity: there was a bodhi tree growing up through the roof, and the cracked walls inside were bare except for a few photographs of *tudong* bhikkhus, like Venerable Ajahn Mun. To be in the presence of such images of austerity and dedication to Dhamma practice was very encouraging. This was the right place, sure enough.

We walked on down to the rocky seashores, the beaches and the sparkling water. We decided to make the best use of the situation by separating and practising on our own most of each day. I had already resolved to fast for the five days that we'd be out there, because whenever I fast then I find that this gives a clarity to my mind, and a greater refinement to my attention. The physical energies calm down and level out and there is less need to sleep.

The weather was beautiful. December in Thailand is a lovely time of year, hot but not stuffy and sticky; and then being on an island there were pleasant breezes, so it was quite idyllic. At night it was warm and balmy and I would sit underneath the measureless stars meditating with the moon as my only companion. Time stretched itself out and went to rest....

So after a few days of this I was getting pretty blissed out. Then, I think it was on the third clear day, I came across a beautiful old wooden palace structure that was half burnt down, set in grounds with frangipani trees – and that was quite amazing. It was near the ruined temple, and exploring further I found a cave which opened into the ground. You could walk down inside this great cleft in the ground, which then opened out to reveal long galleries where you could do walking meditation, and niches in the rock where you could sit and meditate. Then you could go down even further until you couldn't see or hear anything; so you could be completely enfolded in the earth's womb. A hermit's dream!

I thought, 'This is amazing, this is really wonderful!' And it was the day of the full moon. My mind immediately constructed the evening confrontation with Mara: I was near the ruined temple, so I could sit there with Ajahn Mun, or I could go down into the cave and practise, or I could do walking meditation out under the frangipani trees with the cool evening breezes blowing and the full moon beaming down. 'This is it,' I thought, 'this is going to be the night when I really get into some samadhi.'

I was feeling very light, almost skipping up the slope with expectation, when I noticed some people coming along – which was kind of strange. They were all dressed in white; then I recognized that it was one of the anagarikas from the monastery in Siraja we'd been staying at, and he had some lay women with him who were also dressed in white. I quickly realized that they must have come to see us; but I didn't want to be bothered with polite conversation – particularly as I couldn't speak the language. However, they'd seen me: I couldn't ignore that, so I decided to make the best of it, come over, be nice, and hopefully it wouldn't last too long. We sat down by a big bodhi tree outside the ruined temple and they had one of those refrigerated boxes with some Coca Cola in it, so I accepted a bottle and drank some. They started asking questions and talking and I couldn't get very much of what they were saying. I just smiled and said I didn't understand and thought that sooner or later Ajahn Gavesako would happen along. Then he could talk to them, and I could go off and sit somewhere and get into some samadhi.

But somewhere in the back of my mind was an anxious voice: 'Why have they come? I wonder what it is?'

Then Ajahn Gavesako came along. I sat with him for a while, but he seemed quite at ease listening and talking to them, so I thought: 'Well I'll just move off.' I started to slip away; but as I was slipping away he turned around and said: 'Oh, Tuhn Sucitto, pack your bag, will you? We're going back.'

My mind stopped: 'Back, what?' He said, 'We're going back to Siraja.' And I said, 'What for? What are we going back for?' Suddenly my evening of samadhi dropped away. 'Oh, they've invited us.' I looked at him questioningly, and he added, 'I don't know what for. It doesn't matter. They've invited us so we'd better go. It wouldn't be polite to refuse.'

At that point something in me stopped. I turned round and walked off and went to where my bowl bag was and packed my alms bowl with my mind going: 'What do they want? What are we doing? I suppose we're going back to chant something or another, do some ritual. Why can't we stay here? We came here for a few days. We were going to go back in a couple of days anyway. We came here for a few days to *practise* and now we've got to go back to the town. What for? What do they want?' But I knew enough to recognize that resistance in the mind and not to follow it. So I packed my bag. We walked back from that haven to a road where they'd got a motorbike taxi to give us a ride out to the little harbour village. We waited there. I stared glumly at the sea, and then when the ferry came we all packed into it. The boat lingered for a few minutes, then turned and carried us away from the Noble Elephant back to the reeking harbour of Siraja.

We returned to the temple in the city not knowing what for. I went to my kuti, unpacked my bag and sat there waiting for something to happen. And I sat and waited; and nothing happened except the sounds of the city swelled as the duskfall turned into night. Sounds of the traffic, sounds of the world – and I had to listen to it as night turned into day. And it being Christmas Eve and Thai people, Christians as well as Buddhists, enjoying loud music, there were lots of loud Christmas songs – in English. Perhaps it was because they were in English that it didn't seem to matter what they were about, because they weren't even Christmas carols that you could be *inspired* by. What came rolling into my kuti was Christmas Muzak, like 'White Christmas' and 'Rudolph the Red-Nosed Reindeer' – again and again. I sat there in the night and I sat there in the morning; listening, waiting and listening to 'Rudolph the Red-Nosed Reindeer', remembering the full moon, the ruined temple, Ajahn Mun, and samadhi.

But I did listen; and something in me got the point. Something in me stopped resisting and became at one with the way things are. 'Rudolph the Red-Nosed Reindeer' is quite a reasonable song actually, when you listen to it a few times; it's got a moral to it. And when something in me let go and listened to the sounds of the world, it seemed there was a vibrant silence behind it all. And the silence behind the sound of the world seemed to encompass and listen to everything. Profound or petty or inane, no sound could stain the silence of the listening mind; and in that acceptance was timeless compassion.

Nobody came for us; nor did anyone come to take us anywhere. They didn't want me to give a talk, do any chanting, bless anything, go anywhere, say anything. Maybe they were worried that we were getting lonely. Perhaps they thought we were not getting enough to eat; I expect the whole event arose out of compassion. But in the end I was grateful. Whatever the Law or compassionate Bodhisattva that arranges these events – I have a lot to thank them for. They've always managed to catch me out; always turned me away from my attachments, and ideas of practice to make me listen to the way things are. Their emissaries are everywhere. They never let up.

And perhaps I learnt something about the Noble Elephant, the symbol of Dhamma practice. The Buddha himself is likened to the elephant: it's the symbol of the unstoppable aspiration to Nibbana that keeps going through anything. It is with such an aspiration that a *tudong* monk establishes his practice – he inclines to be enduring, to be resilient, and to be tested by wild and lonely places. In fact for me it's always been a great pleasure to go to remote places, where I could be alone and independent. Yet I've also noticed that when I interpret the aspiration too literally, a mahout climbs on the back of the Noble Elephant. This mahout is always saying things like: 'I'm going to get into jhana tonight. This is the real place for practice, if I could stay in this place forever, I'd really develop.' And he's always asking the practice to come up with something fancy; like a mahout that wants his elephant to dance and prance and perform tricks. He's always been a burden, this mahout; and as long as he's driving the elephant I've never felt *that* satisfied, even in blissful circumstances. Instead my attitudes get caught up in trying to prove or attain or hold on to something – a rather self-conscious striving that finally does not lead to coolness, detachment or liberation.

Of course, when one lives as a bhikkhu there are chances to undertake austerities and live alone sometimes, but the basic standard always entails a relationship with the society. The life is one of dependence; it's an interface. Yet if the Buddha established the bhikkhu life for liberation then we should trust the opportunity for selflessness that it presents. It's a bumpy ride at times, but I've learned to appreciate the tests of Sangha life, and the enigmatic compassion of The Way It Is: they always create predicaments where I *have* to let go.

When I came down from my kuti on Christmas Eve morning, Ajahn Gavesako was reading a newspaper. 'It says here there are four babies born in the world *every second!*' 'Better get used to group practice,' I commented.

Sometimes we need austerities, sometimes we need isolation, and sometimes it takes a Red-Nosed Reindeer to awaken us from ourselves.

VENERABLE MUNINDO

Venerable Munindo (Keith Morgan) was born in 1951, and brought up in Morrinsville, New Zealand (North Island). He is the son of a Presbyterian lay preacher, and grandson of two ordained preachers.

He first came across Buddhism while reading Psychology at Waikato University. On moving to Australia in 1972, he met some bhikkhus from the Sydney Thai Vihara; while living in northern New South Wales he attended a meditation retreat with Ajahn Khantipalo.

He left Australia in 1973 bound for Indonesia, with the idea of ultimately reaching Japan to practise Zen. He taught English for a while in Bangkok and met Ajahn Sumedho and some Western monks from Wat Bovornives, where he eventually decided to become a samanera. He received *upasampada* there from Phra Somdet Ñanasaṁvara in 1974, and spent his first *vassa* with Ajahn Thate at Wat Hin Mark Peng, on the Laotian border.

After spending some time spent in a Bangkok hospital with serious health problems, he met Ajahn Sumedho again, and went to Wat Pah Pong. He was reordained there by Ajahn Chah in 1975.

Ill health caused a return to New Zealand for six months in 1979. During his time there, interest grew – both in Auckland and Wellington – in having monks living locally on a more permanent basis.

In 1980 he travelled to England to join the community at Chithurst; three years later, he was given the responsibility of establishing a vihara in Devon, in the south-west of England. Presently, he lives at Chithurst, assisting the abbot with teaching and training of new monks.

THE WORK OF AWARENESS

The following teaching is taken from a Friday night talk given by Venerable Munindo at Dhammaloka Buddhist Centre in Perth, during a visit to Bodhinyana Monastery of Western Australia.

The Middle Way means gently bearing things exactly as they are in their raw condition.

IT HAS BEEN VERY PLEASANT spending time with Ajahn Jagaro after not having seen each other for eight years. We've been talking over some of the developments that have taken place in practice and in our various communities. A rewarding reflection has come out of this as to just how steadily the Path does develop.

It's wonderful to see how the quality of effort that we are able to make in practice naturally grows. I remember how, when I was first ordained in Thailand, the formal 'going for refuge' and 'taking precepts' didn't mean very much to me – *Buddham saranam gacchami, Dhammam saranam gacchami, Sangham saranam gacchami.* ... But although this formality didn't mean much to me then, I was attracted to these teachings because they spoke somehow, in a meaningful way, of 'True Refuge'.

My first contact and inspiration with Buddhism had come from reading a book at university. I had a feeling at the time of, 'Great! there *is* something real – something of true quality which doesn't require compromising what I feel most deeply to be right.' And that was wonderful. It often is this way in the beginning when we make contact with something we can really trust in; we have a wonderful feeling about our discovery.

Then we find the Teaching says that realizing this 'true quality', or to make this quality real in one's life, requires the cultivation of awareness. We are already 'kind of' aware, but our awareness doesn't do what it needs to do, which is to see the facts clearly. The Buddha said that when we see the facts of life – when we see what *is*, as it is – then there are no more problems. The Buddha had no problems because he could always see the facts. If it's not like that for us, then it's not because of life, but because of the way we see it; and that's a very helpful reflection. When I'm having problems, I can consider: the Buddha's Way meant he had no problems, whereas 'my way' means I have. Therefore, one way has to go: either 'my way' or the Buddha's Way. So we take up this training, or the Way of Dhamma, to be free from 'my way'.

And this way of Dhamma begins with this first sense of trust; we feel that Truth *is* accessible, and verifiable to us as human beings. We don't have to wait until we die until we know what's what.

We often find in life, that we are faced with a difficult situation which we want to work with, but we're not up to it. The point of such meetings as this is to actually do something about our ability to work; we have awareness, and we are choosing to work *with* it. We are not just *using* awareness as we do in daily life, but we have set this time aside to directly cultivate it; to sit, to be still, to train the mind.

When our community in England first moved to Chithurst House, it was not an easy situation. One hundred and twenty acres of forest had been given to us, with a lake and an old derelict mansion. But the local council said we had to apply for 'change of use'. So that was done – but the answer was 'No!' So there we were with a wonderful forest in beautiful West Sussex and a potentially ideal house to live in, and yet . . . .

Fortunately, because of a technical point, we were able to apply again; but it meant we had to wait for many months to know the result. There was tremendous doubt; would we be able to stay or not? You could get caught up in the doubt and not do any work, thinking, 'Well, they might throw us out. What's the point?' Or, you could deny doubt, work like a Trojan and get angry at anybody who dared to display any doubt. The training, however, is about seeing just the facts – and thankfully, Ajahn Sumedho was very clear about that. The fact, then, was that that particular situation was very doubtful – uncertain. So with right awareness, with balanced awareness, we could simply bear that uncomfortable feeling. We could bear the feeling of insecurity or doubt.

Insecurity is a very unpleasant feeling. When we are children and feel that way, we seek reassurance from mum and dad. Then as we grow up, we see this feeling of insecurity as a fact of life, and learn to abide in the knowledge of the insecurity of *all* existence; that is, if we really grow up! If we don't really grow up, we find substitutes for our parents: a partner, possessions, belief systems, philosophies and so on.

Our training is to actually *feel* this insecurity, and see it as 'just like this'. But without being balanced we cannot do it. In those early days at Chithurst, it was 'just like that', but there was a real temptation to get caught in an extreme position of either indulging in doubt or repressing it.

In the Buddhist Way, it is clearly stated that the two extremes of 'blindly believing' on the one hand, and 'repression and denial' on the other, are false. The way that is Real is the Middle Way – the way of gently bearing things, exactly as they are, in their raw condition. To do this, we have to train the mind until we are no longer pushing and pulling at the states that we experience.

Pushing and pulling is the way of contending. And it's very easy to contend with life when it's not going the way that 'I' think it should. There was a very difficult period in my training in Thailand after I had already been a monk for about four years. As a result of a motor bike accident I had had before I was ordained, and a number of years of sitting in bad posture, my knees seized up. The doctors in Bangkok said it was severe arthritis, but nothing that a small operation couldn't fix. They said it would take two or three weeks. But after two months and three operations I was still hardly walking. There had been all kinds of complications: scar tissue, three lots of general anaesthetic and the hot season was getting at me; my mind was really in a state. I was thinking: 'My whole life as a monk is ruined. Whoever heard of a Buddhist monk who can't sit cross-legged.' Every time I saw someone sitting cross-legged I'd feel angry. I was feeling terrible, and my mind was saying, 'It shouldn't be like this; the doctor shouldn't have done it like that; the monks' rules shouldn't be this way....' It was really painful, physically and mentally. I was in a *very* unsatisfactory situation.

Then I heard that Ajahn Chah was coming down to Bangkok. I thought if I went to see him he might be able to help in some way. His presence was always very uplifting. When I visited him I couldn't bow properly; he looked over at me and asked, 'What are you up to?' I began to complain: 'Oh Luang Por,' I said, 'It's not supposed to be this way. The doctors said two weeks and it has been two months....' I was really wallowing. With a surprised expression on his face he said to me, very powerfully: 'What do you mean, it *shouldn't* be this way? If it *shouldn't* be this way, it *wouldn't* be this way!'

That really did something to me. I can't describe how meaningful that moment was. He pointed to exactly what I was *doing* that was creating the problem. There was no question about the fact of the pain; the problem was my denying that fact, and that was something I was *doing*. This is not just a theory. When someone offers us the reflection of exactly what we are doing, we are incredibly grateful, even if at the time we feel a bit of a twit.

The pushing away is the distortion of awareness that makes problems out of life. Life can be very painful, but with right awareness there can be a discerning of the facts. When awareness, or mindfulness, matures into truth-discerning awareness (*satipañña*), we can bear the state we are experiencing and discern the facts. With intelligence free to consider what can be done and our human sensitivity unhindered, we don't have to deny what we feel – we can learn from life.

But if our ability to feel is numbed, if our hearts are closed, intelligence simply can't operate. We can go through so many difficult situations in life, thinking: 'Wow! I survived that one. I'll never have to go through that again,' yet before long we do. So whether we learn or not has very much to do with just how accurate our awareness is. It depends on whether we are working with 'right awareness', or the common-or-garden-variety awareness. This practice then is to train awareness – to balance it, to gentle it, to tame it, until the pushing and pulling tendencies are gone.

Just as we make problems out of difficult experiences, we can also make problems out of pleasant ones. There was an occasion when I was in New Zealand and visiting a good friend who used to be a monk with us in England. Now he is a doctor in Christchurch. He spends a lot of time in the very beautiful mountains of the South Island. At his invitation I joined him for a few days walking in the Alps. I hadn't been in the mountains for a long time. The air was good, the weather was good and it was particularly nice to be walking with a good friend. We spent time trekking, walking, talking over practice, sitting meditation... it was wonderful. There was one morning I remember vividly. We had left very early the forest hut where we'd spent the night. It was dawn as we walked down a big stony mountain river bed. The magic light of sunrise was tipping the snowcapped mountains gold. It was so beautiful... drinking the stream water, breathing crisp mountain air, and being in good company. Then something in my mind started up.... a feeling started arising... and it was beginning to spoil the situation. So gently paying attention to that... carefully turning towards it and being with that feeling... the constriction of energy that was taking place... I could see there was a feeling of ... trying to hold on to the experience – the experience of simple human enjoyment. I was saying to myself, 'This is how it *should* be.' In that moment, I could see how I was creating a problem. I was already beginning to imagine how it would be back in the English drizzle saying, 'It *shouldn't* be this way.'

So even around pleasure we create problems by not relating directly, truly; by not relating to that which is true, but relating to that which is false, or to our fantasies. With pleasure, we can feel afraid of losing it, and fantasize in an attempt to hold on to it. With pain, we tend to dwell in memories of when it wasn't there, in an attempt to avoid it. This is how it often is in broken relationships. (And death is a kind of broken relationship.) Rather than seeing the fact of the pain, there is a tendency to go into memories of 'how it used to be' or fantasize about 'how it could be'. That is dwelling in what's not real.

There is a verse in the Dhammapada:

Mistaking the false for the real, and the real for the false,
   we remain stuck in the false.
Seeing the real as real, and the false as false,
   we attain to the Truly Real.

To be able to do the work of seeing the false as false and the real as real, we need to cultivate this truth-discerning awareness. We need to operate in a mode whereby we can accept the offerings of life and death completely, whole-heartedly, and discern the facts – the Truth.

So being whole-hearted means being wholly and completely sensitive; not being sensitive merely to what we like, which is 'my way', and denying what we don't like. The Buddha's Way means being single-minded about our consideration of life. And it results in an agility of mind which is intelligence; the mind is not merely conditioned; it is free to perform its proper function.

This is the training, and we can be very grateful that we've been offered this training. The Buddha described this Way as being 'Well-Expounded', *Svakkhata Dhamma.* In other words, he said, 'You've got what you need to do what needs to be done.' We don't have to make shots in the dark hoping that we'll come across something meaningful. Here we have a complete training – the training of body, speech and mind. We cultivate moral responsibility and work at developing the mind. We make the effort to concentrate the mind and really be in the present. All the difficulties and pitfalls that we experience along the way, we share with each other. We have Good Companions – *Kalyanamitta,* members of the Sangha, and Dhamma friends, who can come together for discussion and reflection – listening to talks and going on retreats. We can actually do what the Buddha wanted us to do.

The quality of trust we have in the beginning is wonderful. It says: 'Yes, there is something to be realized. Life isn't merely an ordeal that we tolerate until we die. There is a true quality that can be seen and known.' And then, having given ourselves to the training, we find that we begin to go beyond the habitual tendencies of pushing and pulling at the experiences of pleasure and pain. And we continue until we come upon a new way of seeing. We see in a way that we've never seen before. We have a new perspective of things. 'Trust' is now verified. We need no longer be concerned with doubt about the possibility of the Way; we simply get on with it.

All the training we do, including the traditions that we use, are for this purpose. They make our life situations workable. Anger becomes workable; greed, jealousy, pleasure, pain, all become something to help us grow in the direction of True Understanding. 'I go for refuge to Dhamma – the way things *actually* are' takes on a new meaning for us.

Then finally, and thankfully, there are beings in the world who teach from the perspective of *complete* trust. The Buddha's Teachings come from the perspective of complete trust. That is where life itself is something that we give ourselves into with an attitude of complete trust. There is no longer any doubt, any confusion, any despair. All that remains is complete trust in Dhamma.

*   *   *

QUESTION: *Would you comment on the statement: 'Accepting things the way they are is a passive avoidance of taking responsibility.'*

ANSWER: If it's avoidance of taking responsibility, then it has nothing at all to do with the spiritual life. This Way means becoming completely responsible – it means developing the ability to respond whole-heartedly and single-mindedly to whatever situation we may be in. That is far from being passive. It's being perfectly active. It means acting in a complete and perfect way – doing what is appropriate to the situation. That may mean doing nothing. It may mean doing something. The principle means whatever you do, do completely. Then you can be truly responsible for the outcome. Our sensitivity is right there with us and intelligence isn't hindered; you can say or act as is called for. If nothing is called for, we don't do anything. Even if we get it wrong, which often happens, and we become caught in the false, as soon as we see it, we're real again: no pushing or pulling, just feeling it as it is. This is the vision of the practice.

VENERABLE PURISO

Venerable Puriso (Bruce Evans) was born in Melbourne, Australia in 1951. As a young man he became involved in the music business and made a record. Through contact with a Zen teacher in Melbourne he was inspired to go to Japan to study Zen.

En route, he stopped over in Bangkok and met some Western bhikkhus, but was put off training in the Theravada tradition because of the restrictions on music in the monks' discipline. Nonetheless, he decided to attend a Vipassana meditation retreat in Nong Khai. While attending the retreat his guitar was stolen. This made him decide to abandon his plans to train in Japan, and he started to investigate more closely what opportunities might be available in Thailand.

Having heard about Ajahn Chah, he visited Wat Pah Pong, and eventually took *upasampada* there in 1975, with Ajahn Chah as his preceptor. In 1982 he went back to Australia with Venerable Jagaro to help found a monastery in Perth. After some time he returned to Thailand. He is now senior incumbent at Wat Wana Potiyahn (Wat Keurn), not far from Wat Pah Pong, and close to the Lao/Cambodian border, where he is actively engaged in working to preserve the dwindling forests in the area. This work was featured in a very successful television documentary, which was broadcast nationwide in Thailand.

SEEING IN THE LIGHT OF DHAMMA

In the meditation monasteries of North-East Thailand it is a tradition for the village people to spend the new moon and full moon uposatha days in the monastery. They keep the eight precepts and practise meditation alongside the monks and nuns until dawn of the following day. On such evenings a Dhamma talk is given especially to encourage laity. The following talk, translated from the Thai by the speaker, was given by Venerable Puriso during the Rainy-Season Retreat (Vassa) of 1987.

**When you bring light into a dark place,
the darkness disappears, no matter how long
the darkness has been there.**

FOR YOU WHO HAVE COME TO THE MONASTERY, leaving your homes for the observance day, it is a good opportunity to stop and reflect on your lives. Where are you going? Are you travelling the worldly path or the path of Dhamma? If you are travelling the path of Dhamma, are you making progress? In the practice of Dhamma, one should constantly try to improve oneself; don't just go about things in a perfunctory way – move ahead. To make the Dhamma meaningful, you have to make it relevant to your life, reflecting on your actions in the light of Dhamma.

For example, when developing *sati*, recollection. In any one day, how much time do you spend with *sati*, being aware of yourself? We develop *sati* in our meditation practice. At first, one may only be able to keep one's attention on the breath for two or three seconds before it wanders. Especially if you don't establish your mind when sitting, you may not even follow the breath for even two or three seconds. You may end up just sitting there, passing the time away.

When sitting in meditation, you should really, consciously, sit in meditation. What is our task when sitting meditation? We must bring the breath to mind, to recollect on, contemplate around, or notice the in- and out-breaths. This is developing the ability to recollect or be mindful – *sati*. Using repetition, we can improve our ability in this area.

With all the practices in the forest monastery here, there is room for improvement and refinement. What are our practices here? Firstly, for instance, there is eating one meal a day. This is one of our basic practices. In forest monasteries this standard should be observed firmly. Another one is the practice of not lying down in the evenings of the observance days. For those who have the strength, this should also be observed – although if one's health is not good, one may not be able to go all through the night. Even so, one can still make the effort to be especially diligent on that night.

Listening to Dhamma is another one of our practices. Listening to Dhamma is something one must train in. If one has never listened to Dhamma, one won't really know how to do it. One's mind will wander and one will get caught up in thoughts of criticism or praise, approval or disapproval, and so on. As for those who have trained in listening to Dhamma, when they hear the Dhamma they feel pleasure. Likewise, if we can practise the Dhamma in our everyday lives, we should experience lightness and ease as a result. We should experience the 'disbanding' or 'dissolving' of suffering. The suffering of this world arises through clinging and attachment. The world is the sphere of 'me' and 'mine'.

Now in this world there are many people, so it's necessary to share things around. But in fact, there isn't much sharing, there's more grabbing going on. People are struggling against each other to make a living, raise a family, set themselves up securely, and so on. In other words, they're suffering. Generally speaking, people manage to get by, but there are times when things get rough, problems arise in the form of disputes, quarrels, fighting, and so on. It's just as if people were blinded by darkness.

So what should we do? We must listen to the Dhamma, contemplate the Dhamma. We must learn to look at all these things in the light of Dhamma, bringing light into our minds. When you bring light into a dark place, the darkness disappears.

No matter how long the darkness has been there, it dissipates the instant we bring light into that place. The 'light' here is the understanding of things in the light of Dhamma. What is the light of Dhamma? When we know how to let go of 'me' and 'mine', and see things as they are – this is seeing things in the light of Dhamma.

For instance, in Buddhism we talk about the 'Eight Worldly Dhammas': gain and loss, praise and criticism, fame and obscurity, happiness and suffering. These are the things most people are running after or from. People look for wealth and possessions. Praise is another thing people look for. We like to hear people say we are good and clever. Words like that please us. If we hear words of criticism or abuse, we don't feel so good. Another kind of worldly Dhamma is status. Some people aren't so interested in wealth as such, but they like rank and power. Politicians may spend lots of money to get political power and position.

If we look into all these worldly Dhammas, we will notice that they all tend to swell up one's self-image. However, the practice of Dhamma tends to work towards cutting it down, towards giving up pride. 'Self building' is contrary to the way of things, because in the end we lose all those things anyway.

I've noticed the monkeys here in the forest. Sometimes I've seen them playing a game, something like 'King of the Castle'. One of the monkeys will run to the top of a termite mound. He's the King of the Castle. Then all the other monkeys down below will compete with each other to pull him down and get up there themselves. All of the monkeys want to get on top, they want to be big, they want to show their stuff. But being on top doesn't necessarily guarantee happiness. In fact, the monkey on top of the mound suffers more than all the others. He's got to be constantly on guard against the other monkeys jumping up and pulling him off the mound. The others are much better off, they've got nothing to lose.

There's something we can learn from this, too. 'Make yourself small.' To say 'Make yourself small' doesn't mean to make yourself stupid, lazy or cowardly, but to know how to let go: to be humble, respectful, easily contented and appreciative.

These four qualities are contrary to the normal way of the world. In the world, people don't usually aim for these sorts of things – they normally seek to make themselves big. The Buddha said this is contrary to nature.

So whatever practice is a vehicle to help us let go of 'me' and 'mine' is a correct practice, as well as being the way to happiness. This is because letting go is happiness; clinging is suffering. Regarding this point here, one who has never studied or thought about the Dhamma won't like to hear it, because most people tend to cling. There are many things people cling to as being their own. Seeing things as being one's own in an absolute sense is called 'clinging'. If one isn't clinging, one will see that 'our' things are ours only in a relative sense. As long as supporting conditions are there, then those things will also be there; but when supporting factors no longer exist, then those things also cease. Thinking in this way is thinking in the light of Dhamma. And thinking in the light of Dhamma will make us cool and peaceful; we will experience the disbanding of clinging. When clinging is disbanded, we will experience lightness.

That we come to practise in the monastery is not so that we can simply run away from home, but so that we can step back a bit from our everyday lives and look at things more clearly. If we were to practise only at home, there would be difficulties. One might feel embarrassed to sit or walk meditation. But all of you who come to the monastery come with the single intention of studying and practising the religion. So you can all relax. If somebody wants to practise walking meditation, that person won't have to feel embarrassed or afraid that people will look askance at him, because walking meditation is one of our duties here. If you tried doing walking meditation in the market place, they might think you were crazy, and lock you up! So we come to practise in the monastery where we can relax, practise meditation, read Dhamma books or simply spend the day quietly. Keeping the precepts is already a meritorious action, because actually it's quite difficult to do, especially the eight precepts. If one keeps the eight precepts, one is living like a renunciant, especially here in this monastery where it's very peaceful, and removed from the bustle of household life. Living here for a day and a night is like ordaining for a day and a night. If you were to try living like this at home, it wouldn't be easy – sounds of radio, television, people coming and going – these things don't help meditation practice.

However, having come to stay here, we should look into suffering. There will be suffering arising within our bodies and minds. Our duty is to understand the truth of suffering. What does suffering arise from, how does it arise? We must study these things. The Buddha taught, 'Suffering is something that should be recognized,' but most people don't want to recognize it. If suffering arises, the only thing they can think of doing is to try to run away from it. They don't want to look into it. They are not real Dhamma practisers. A Dhamma practiser must look into problems as they arise in order to understand their causes.

Sometimes, some incident may arise which we instantly react to – for instance, when people criticize us. But if we look into what they say, we may find some truth there. Our getting angry was simply a defence-reaction based on fear. If we accept what they say, that is, we recognize their right to say what they wish, then no incident arises.

If we practise so as not to give rise to any 'incidents' in our lives, we will have some peace. If any incidents do arise, we dare to look into them in the light of Dhamma, with openness, clarity and honesty. But seeing things in the light of Dhamma is not easy. We have our habits. This is what makes seeing in the light of Dhamma so difficult. We see things not as they are but coloured by our habitual reactions and value judgements.

We must depend on Dhamma practice to further train ourselves. We must develop moral discipline (sila) and mental discipline (samadhi) in order to give rise to understanding (pañña). Sila and samadhi are the tools with which we calm our actions, speech and thoughts. If our actions, speech and thoughts are not restrained, everything is agitated, we can't see things the way they are. In other words, we can't see in the light of Dhamma. We must firmly take hold of the practices which the Buddha has bequeathed us: moral precepts, the *dhutaṅga* practices, making merit and giving offerings; these are all tools in our practice. They give us the strength to overcome the hindrances and develop clarity.

How can we give up hindrances? Take the example of giving offerings. Whether offering of material goods or offering of one's time and energy, these are all aspects of *dana,* and they are one way of giving up mental hindrances and cleansing our mind. Don't think that making offerings is in order to go to heaven. That's not a sure thing. If one makes offerings and yet does bad actions, one may end up going to hell. Making merit through good deeds and making offerings are done in order to cleanse one's mind. You can see the fruit of your action in the present moment, you don't have to go looking off into a future life. Future lives are an uncertainty, we should consider this life. If you give offerings wholeheartedly, without a trace of doubt or regret, giving fully with one's whole heart, one will experience happiness right there, a sense of well-being and fulfilment. Right there is the fruit of giving, you don't have to look for it in the future.

Keeping the precepts is the same. If one keeps the precepts wholeheartedly, without doubts on one hand or self-pride on the other, one will experience a feeling of strength in one's heart. The mind will be firm and strong. If one takes such a mind and trains it further in concentration practice, that firmness will increase until the mind becomes unified. This is our path of practice.

This is how the forest monasteries teach the Dhamma. They teach us to practise the Dhamma, to actually put it into practice, to the best of our ability, and to see the fruits of the practice in the present, right before your eyes. For instance, if you practise meditation and calm the mind, the fruit of your efforts will be plainly there before you. You don't have to think of practising meditation for some future result, you can see the fruit right there. Goodness is its own reward. This point is one that people don't seem to understand. They see people going to the monastery for years and never getting rich, so they conclude that they've done good deeds and received no result. This is a misunderstanding. If one really does virtuous deeds, there must be virtue within one at that time. The fruit of the action is right there within one. The same applies to bad actions. Sometimes we may see others doing bad things and seeming to get away with it, and so conclude that they've done bad actions and received no bad result. This is still not seeing clearly.

In Buddhism we say, 'Good actions bring good results, bad actions bring bad results.' This isn't a theory, an idea, an ideal, or some form of wishful thinking – it is the way things are, whether one sees it or not. People who commit evil acts become evil people. Their minds, their speech and their actions become evil. This is the result of their evil actions, in keeping with the Buddha's instruction, 'We are the owners of our kamma.'

Moreover, good and bad actions reap future results as well, such as when a thief steals something. At the time of stealing, he may even feel pleasure of a sort – even if it is a shoddy sort of pleasure – and it may last for many days. He may get a lot of money and spend it lavishly, but when the police catch him, all that pleasure he experienced is as nothing – it disappears without a trace – leaving him alone with the consequences of his actions. This is the fruit of bad kamma. If we really practise and contemplate, we should see that this is so.

When I went to Australia with Ajahn Jagaro, the day we arrived at Perth Airport we were approached by a man as we were going through Customs. He was a little drunk, but he must have been something of a philosopher as well. Seeing us monks aroused his curiosity, so he came to ask about our religion. We told him we were Buddhists.

'Oh, Buddhists. You revere the Buddha, is that right?'

'Yes.'

'They tell me, the Buddha was such a pure being, living such an exemplary life, giving up himself for the sake of others, revered by the world as a great sage . . . . But eventually he died, didn't he?'

'Yes, that's right.'

'Now suppose we take the example of someone who committed untold evil – such as Hitler, for example. He was responsible for the deaths of so many people, so much suffering, so many heinous deeds... but in the end, he also died, right?'

'Yes, that's right.'

'Well then, what's the difference? One man practises so virtuously, one commits so much evil – but in the end they both died just the same. What's the use of virtue, if that's the case?'

I answered, 'They both died, it's true, but it wasn't the same thing. The Buddha understood death. He lived his life fully aware of the fact of death and was unshaken by it. When the time came for him to die, he died peacefully, without doubts, without regrets, having lived a 'true' life, one that was lived in accordance with the truth.

'Hitler, on the other hand, didn't understand death. His life was lived with fear and suspicion, his mind was wrought with untold sufferings and a view that was ignorant of the truth, which is why he could commit such evil actions anyway. His life was lived out of fear, and he died in confusion and darkness. His life was full of ignorance and falsehood. This is the important difference: one of them understood, the other didn't.'

This is the important point. We Buddhists should have this understanding in our hearts. What does 'Buddha' mean? *Buddha* means 'knowing', *Buddho* means 'the one who knows'. This Buddhist Religion is the religion of knowing and understanding the way things really are.

Now, the knowledge of the Buddha and the enlightened disciples is not the knowledge of so much – it's basically to know oneself. If you want to be a true Buddhist, you must cultivate that knowing in your heart. This knowing is not like worldly knowledge, which is an amassing of facts and ideas. It is simply to know ourselves.

If you know how to practise like this, then it's just like planting a

Bodhi-tree in your mind. All the bad, unwholesome qualities will be like fertilizer to feed the Bodhi-tree, the tree of knowing. You will be able to use the defilements of mind as objects of awareness, as vehicles to see the true state of your mind, and seeing the true state of greed, hatred and delusion.

For example, if you happen to get angry, then know that anger has arisen. Don't fool yourself by saying, 'No, I'm not angry, it's just that so-and-so is such a dirty rat....' Sometimes when we are angry, we fail to recognize it because we put all our attention onto the object of anger rather than on our own minds. We are always watching others, rarely ourselves.

The Buddha said that, no matter what happens, accept it and investigate it. Such as when anger arises: know that this is anger and investigate it. How does it feel to be angry? Do you feel happy when you're angry? If you do this, then you are looking at things in the light of Dhamma. Eventually you will learn to let go of anger, because you will know that it causes suffering. If it causes suffering, why cling to it?

But this is easy to say... hard to do. Even so, listening to a discourse can remind us of our direction and encourage us to practise. If we practise hard not to get deluded by the conditions of mind, then we are behaving as real Buddhists.

*   *   *

It hadn't rained for many days. Walking around, I saw the forest parched, some trees seemed to be dying. Now that it's rained, the frogs are all out revelling in the water. They find themselves a puddle, and croak away so happily – they probably think those puddles are always going to be there. But when the rain stops in no long time they will all dry up, and the frogs will be dying of the heat.

Our human lives are similar. When conditions are conducive, we are able to live fairly comfortably. When conditions change, we may not be able to continue. These days, people seem intent on destroying nature. They don't seem to realize that human beings are parts of nature, born of nature, just like those frogs. If human

beings destroy nature, it is just like destroying themselves –
because we don't exist separate and above nature, we live
dependent on it, as part of it. Destroy nature and we destroy
ourselves.

So, on that note, I'll finish off the Dhamma talk. I hope that some
things I've said may be of use. At least you may have some good
food for reflection, so that you take what you've heard and
examine it, using it to develop your own wisdom.

VENERABLE KITTISARO

Venerable Kittisaro (Randolph Weinberg) was born in 1952 in Tennessee. He went to a military high school and excelled at wrestling, becoming Mid-South Wrestling Champion five times, and winner of the 'National Tournament' championship. At Princeton University he studied History and Philosophy of Science, and graduated with high honours (Phi Beta Kappa) in 1974. He intended to go on to study medicine, but studied English at Oxford instead, after winning a Rhodes scholarship. While working on a thesis about Aldous Huxley, he started to yearn for some sense of inner peace.

His search for quiet places took him to the Buddhist Centre at Oakenholt near Oxford. At a retreat there with Dr. Rewata Dhamma, a Burmese monk, he met Dr. Douglas Burns, a disciple of Ajahn Chah. Hearing about Ajahn Chah and Ajahn Sumedho, he decided to go to Thailand to become a monk himself. He became a samanera at Wat Pah Pong in February 1977, and received *upasampada* from Ajahn Chah four months later.

During his second year in Thailand, Venerable Kittisaro contracted typhoid and nearly died. Still not fully recovered, he was called back to the U.S. because of family illness. Instead of returning to Thailand, he went on to England, and joined the monks who were then moving to Chithurst. His physical condition continued to deteriorate, however; eventually he was diagnosed to have Chrone's Disease. After several years of serious illness, his health began to improve slowly, and he has now made a reasonable recovery.

From 1985 to 1988 he was senior incumbent of the Devon Vihara.

CONTEMPLATION AND ACTION

The following questions and answers with Venerable Kittisaro are taken from a public talk given in Bath, and a session with religious education teachers who visited the Devon Vihara – both in 1986.

**When our mind is open and in the state of wonder...
that's the state of love – truly being with something
as it is, whether it is horrible or pleasant.**

Could you outline for us your daily routine?

IN THE MONASTERY WE RISE AT 4 O'CLOCK. From then until about 4.45 a.m., we get energized doing exercise and so on. At 5 o'clock, there is morning chanting, with an offering of candles, incense, flowers and bowing. The idea is to begin the day by offering that which is beautiful. These actions are a way of pointing our whole being towards Buddha, being collected and awake. So we're setting a direction for the day. Then we make the dedication: 'May my life today be of benefit to all beings.'

The sitting meditation that follows is usually for an hour. At 6.30 we clean the house, then have tea and a drink of gruel (like liquidy porridge). I do a reading from the Teachings, or give a talk. Then the monks go on 'almsround' through the villages. As 'alms mendicants', it's our duty just to be visible: not to bother people, not to harass them, but to let it be known there's a monk about. If anybody wants to make offerings or talk to us, then we are available. We now have about fifteen houses in the area where they make regular invitation. So we just walk about quietly with our bowl. We have our meal for the day at 10.30 a.m. This is made up of what's been offered, either on the almsround or by other supporters who have visited the monastery. Then we have a short rest.

In the afternoon there's work. I do a lot of receiving guests and travelling to give talks, leading retreats and study. There's always a lot of work to do on the property. We have tea in the afternoon at about five. Then another service, or chanting, at 7.30 p.m., which anyone can come to. On at least two evenings a week I give a formal talk on some aspect of the teaching. Once a week there's an all-night vigil, when we practise sitting and walking meditation until just before dawn.

It takes years to learn how to live in a community: how to learn to live with one another, how to live as a celibate, how to live with simple possessions. We emphasize learning how to let go of status, seeing it as just a form of self-conceit. For the rest of my life I will always bow to those who have been in the Order longer than I. That doesn't mean I have to believe they're better than I am just because I'm in that relationship to them; that's how the conventional relationship is with those who are senior. I can use the situation to learn to be humble. In a monastery everyone merges; there are no limits on who can be wise! Now I find a sense of beauty in bowing to the elders.

Do lay Buddhists adapt these principles to their situation? ·

There are five principles to follow: refrain from killing, stealing, sexual misconduct, lying and intoxicants. These guidelines enable us to look into our life and see that which causes conflict: to see the impulse which is always wanting something. We look into our heart and see that which exploits and is bound by sexual energy, which doesn't use it wisely. We see the impulse to distort the truth. And recognize how drugs and alcohol are unskilful ways of avoidance. When someone is not living by these principles their ability to endure hardships is wasted away. But if we do accord with them, then the result of that spiritually is that we become able to bear with things. If we're not able to bear with things, we're not able to understand suffering.

What does Buddhism teach about love?

Buddhism teaches that love has to be understood. Generally we attach to an idea of love: love is *liking* something. We tend to use the word very loosely. However, in the Buddhist sense, to really love something means to *allow* it to be, to know it as it is: a willingness to listen and be attentive. When a mother loves her child, she is attentive to that child's needs. That doesn't mean she always likes it – for instance, when the child is screaming and not sleeping at night – but she's willing to *be* with that child. For the mother, the child just *is* the way it is. As I understand it, the Buddha taught that the purest form of love is to not fight something: not struggling against something, but allowing it to live, to be present in our consciousness. Then we can be attentive to it.

Then you say: 'Well, gosh, that seems pretty cold – that won't change the world!' But when you give attention to something without demanding that it be different, that very attentiveness has a profound transforming effect. This is what I found with my own body and illness. For some reason I didn't die, and now I'm at least able to go around and meet people. For many years all I could do was just *be* with the body, be with the discomfort, be with the pain as it was. But allowing all that to be in the mind, just as it was, caring for it – gave so much nourishment.

We find in physics now that they don't talk about an 'objective observer' and 'the observed' any more. Physicists have come around to seeing in terms of 'the participant'. The mere fact of looking at something means you start to change it. Now if you look at someone you love and you see something you don't like and try to make them be different, you're actually forcing – and that can be quite cruel. So the Buddha would say that hatred can never be stilled by hatred. Aversion won't cease by fighting it: only through kindness, through not hating something, can a condition live, and then die, naturally. Hatred has to die a natural death. As soon as we try to kill hatred we actually reproduce it all over the place. And when hatred ceases, love remains.

What do you think about doctrinal statements on such things as how the world began and so on?

They're just endless speculation – even though they may be fun to sit down and talk about! The Buddha had a simile that relates to this. He talked about a man who had been shot by a poisonous arrow. Before allowing the arrow to be removed this man demanded to know: 'Who shot me? What kind of bow was it?

What kind of arrow was it? Which direction did it come from?'
The doctor said: 'If I answer all those questions, you'll be dead.'

People used to come to the Buddha and ask, 'Is the world finite or
infinite? What happens to an enlightened being after they die?'
What was the beginning of the world?', and all of these mar-
vellously intriguing questions. The Buddha said: 'If you talk
about these questions, you're going to be dead, and miss this
wonderful opportunity as a human being to be free.'

We need to be free from ignorance, to *taste* freedom itself –
freedom from imagining that we're a body, freedom from that
which ties us down to the finite. The Buddha's teaching always
comes back to that which frees you from ignorance and suffering.
It's not skilful to spend a lot of time on such doctrinal statements.
Time is precious! Pull out the poisoned arrow. Go straight to the
root of the problem.

*What is the Buddhist attitude to social work and engagement in social
issues – doing practical things to help? Is Buddhism entirely impractical?*

First of all, I think the idea that 'people who are *just*
contemplating don't have any effect on the world' needs to
be considered. I know that in our monastery when someone is
peaceful, it has an effect on the others; when someone is being
very irritable all the time, that also has an effect on the others.

Then there's this idea that a great gap exists between action and
contemplation. Again in physics, they're beginning to see that the
act of looking at something has a tremendous effect. The way we
look at things creates our world, our whole attitude. All our
indignation, all our liking and disliking comes from our attitude.

A Buddhist contemplative approach would be considering
the Four Noble Truths. The First Noble Truth says: 'There is
suffering.' Normally we think, 'I am suffering. I want to get out of
suffering,' and so we focus on hope, on wanting to get out. The
pain looks like something we want to get away from. The Buddha
says you'll *never* get away from it that way. We like to grab hold of
pleasure – but the pleasure changes, because it's a relative truth.

Buddhism swings you right out – the First Noble Truth – to look right *at* pain or unhappiness.

It is the same thing as when Jesus said: 'Pick up your cross.' We've got to bear the cross: the whole symbol of surrendering, rather than using his powers to fly up into the sky. We turn to pain and look right at it, feel it and investigate it: 'What is it?' Notice how thoughts say, 'This is pain, this is horrible, I can't take this any more.' We begin to watch the nature of these ideas that we tack onto the pain: making it *my* pain, and unendurable.

Mysteriously, once we start to look at pain it changes too, because it's not a solid thing. So this is what the physicists are learning: just the act of observing something is actually participating in changing it. By looking at suffering, we're actually part of the transformation of it. Understanding it, standing under it, bearing with it, we become free from false notions of pain and pleasure. By investigating it, already we see it as something that appears to us, and then dispassion arises.

Now, what about the kind of action you're talking about? Buddhists are encouraged to be open and see what needs to be done, but not to look too far away too soon. It's easy to get fired up about doing something 'important', but what about the ordinary things like getting along with our family, and business companions? If we do not have time for these things, then our work becomes misguided. We may be *talking* about harmony and peace, but have not yet dealt with the basic problem.

So yes: as we meditate and learn a proper perspective on things, we learn to do whatever we *can* do. Depending on our abilities and the situation we're in, we dedicate our lives to being of benefit to the whole. As a Buddhist monk there are certain things I can do and certain things I can't. My job as a monk is to learn to live simply: eating very simply, having simple robes, learning to rely on that which is offered. Also learning to be available for whoever comes, to develop a willingness to be interrupted. That's being just one tiny cog in this whole cosmos.

When each person starts to contemplate what Right Speech is, and what Right Livelihood is, they find from their own heart the most appropriate way to be of benefit to the whole. And at the same time, they're not forgetting to be mindful and attentive. Mindfulness is that which sees that what we do is kept in balance – sees that we're not being guided by Wrong View.

It's a slow process maybe, but it encourages each of us to grow up. We learn to use the wisdom we have, to open up from being concerned with *just* this body or *just* this family, or *just* this country, or *just* this political party. If we just take sides with one little group, it can lead to so much trouble. But the open mind simply senses suffering wherever it happens to be, and makes an effort to alleviate it.

Yes, it's a crime that the world has so much suffering in it now. We have so much power and yet we haven't alleviated a lot of the basic problems. But the problems are not going to be solved by trying to force people. They'll be solved by really giving attention to them and each person doing what they can.

Is it really a question of understanding yourself before you can help anybody else?

There's a problem in the logic in that. When you write it down in a sentence it sounds like you have to do all the self-understanding first, and then, after you've become a Buddha, go out and help people; and before that you can't do anything. Really it doesn't work that way. Both aspects work together all the time. In my own case when I was in Thailand I used to feel really good being someone who was helpful in the monastery – helping my teacher, helping all the monks do yoga, always running around doing something 'helpful'. Then when I became ill and unable to do anything, I was totally incapable of being at peace with things. There was no real wisdom. A lot of my action had been coming from desperation. This desperation had actually tainted some of what I was doing.

This is why in Buddhism we always talk about balance, and the importance of having a regular time for real quietude. Just how much time one spends being quiet is up to each person – a minute, or just five minutes of sitting down and being still is useful. Then we can notice the pull of what we think we have to do; the guilt of thinking we're being selfish – or whatever there is. Getting those feelings in perspective – seeing that which is running us around all the time, puts us in a better position for understanding life.

If we wait around until we're perfectly enlightened – I tell you what, I wouldn't be here tonight talking to you all! You'd have to wait until the cows come home, and they wouldn't be coming home! Because there's always another doubt that comes in: maybe I'm not ready, yet.

If the thought comes: 'Am I ready yet?', I *see* that as a thought – right here and now. If, when I'm meditating that thought comes, I see that it has a beginning... 'Am I ready yet?'... and that that thought has an end; and noticing that when that thought ends, there's peace in the mind. When I can see that the thought is just a thought which comes and goes, I can see it as a changing condition in the mind. I don't have to make a problem out of it any more. I don't have to wait for the time when there are no more doubting thoughts. I just know it's a doubting thought and I can offer what I'm able to. This brings forth patience and equanimity. And this is what we can do in an immediate sense.

How many times has someone passed us on the road too quickly and we've let out a whole chain of profanities? So we start with the little things. If we want to be like Jesus and save the world, that's fine, but where have we got to start? The Buddha started with the little things; he said, let's be honest, climb the tree from the bottom, you don't jump into Nibbana, you don't jump into God; you first learn to be patient with what's already happening – like a headache. Then one is building up mindfulness in this present moment.

Is it going to lead to a universal impracticality if we take up Buddhism? ... How do you feel about going into our technological world and making the changes that are needed?

One thing I need to say is that it isn't really for me to make proclamations about what 'Buddhists' think and feel. Are such statements really useful? In Buddhism the whole teaching is about a path towards Awakening. Each of us is seeing this room from a different perspective, and so for me to tell others what they should see or do is basically impossible.

As a general reflection, though, I feel we have tremendous power now to manipulate things. We have the ability to create all sorts of things through science, and we're beginning to understand some of the laws of how materials – what we call the 'aggregate of form' – how these operate. We have great power to change things, to move things, to dig up the earth, to send people to the Moon, to blow up the planet. We have tremendous abilities to produce. Our language and society is all about being productive.

Well, the religious impulse realizes that we have gone too far into the world of manipulating things to become as we want them. There's an idea that if we eradicate enough diseases through this marvellous science then we'll be disease-free, pain-free, trouble-free, and *then* we'll be happy. But that's a materialistic extreme. And when we go to an extreme we only see life as it *could* be – through concepts. There's tremendous power in the desire to create. But this desire to make things be as we want them can also become very cruel. Although we have this tremendous power, we have still hardly moved in our ability to get along with one another – we're still fighting, getting separated, and misunderstanding each other.

So the religious impulse tells us how to appreciate things. It talks about opening the heart. When we were children and went to the seashore we would look at the vastness with our eyes wide open. Wind blowing in... thousands of waves... the roar of the sea... The mind had no way to manipulate that vastness. So when our mind is open, we're just listening and watching. And in that state of wonder, the state of awe, the state of communion, we're *actually* appreciating. Now that's the state of love, the state of truly being with something as it is, whether it's horrible or pleasant. And in *that* state we are a part of the whole thing – we are connected to the whole.

But *that* can also become an extreme! What are we going to do about all that needs to be done if we're attached to being in a state of awe? So it's not a matter of one extreme or the other.

There's nothing good or evil about modern medicine, or nuclear technology, or any of these things. But often the human minds that are using them have become divorced from reality. So rather than make proclamations about what people should do in the active sense, I'd encourage everyone to open up to life... and then we start to see how we actually feel about pain – 'I don't like it.' When compassion arises we are able to *suffer with* others; we actually vibrate with them. We truly realize that they're suffering and then we're simply not inclined to do things that hurt. But if you just tell someone 'don't do that', 'be compassionate', such issuing proclamations is using force. You might get people to act the way you want them to, but there would still be *avijja* – ignorance. So the Buddha taught that the source of the entire problem is ignorance. We point at that, and out of awareness naturally comes forth compassion – that being at one with the whole.

VENERABLE BODHIPALO

Venerable Bodhipalo (Michael Markham) was born in Nottingham, England, in 1948. When he was young, his family moved around quite a lot, and he spent 18 months in Canada when he was eight years old. After leaving school he did various jobs, but was unable to find anything that really interested him; eventually, he decided to go travelling. He went overland through Europe to the Middle East, and on to India and Nepal. In Kathmandu, he read a book about meditation, which sparked off his interest; later, while staying in Benares, he heard about a meditation course being held in Bodh Gaya, and travelled there to attend.

He returned to the U.K. in 1972 and worked on a farm, but, still feeling unable to settle, he went back to India in 1974. At Bodh Gaya he became a samanera, travelling later that year to Wat Pah Pong, where he received bhikkhu ordination. However, uncertain about making a long-term commitment to the Holy Life, he disrobed and returned to the U.K. in 1976. After a short time back in lay life he realized that it still did not suit him, and with fresh resolve he went back to Thailand and received *upasampada* again, this time with Ajahn Chah as preceptor.

He visited the U.K. in 1986 for health reasons, spending a few months at Chithurst Monastery, before setting out on a pilgrimage to the Buddhist holy places in India.

He is currently living in Thailand.

WALKING THROUGH INDIA

Venerable Bodhipalo returned to England from Thailand in 1986, to spend time with his family and at Chithurst Buddhist Monastery. On the journey back to Thailand he decided to undertake a lone pilgrimage in India to the Buddhist holy places. After a few months a letter was received by the community at Chithurst. Here are some extracts.

People told me all the terrible things that might happen ... so I thought of all the good things, and decided to walk to Lumbini.

I LEFT SAVATTHI ON 4TH DECEMBER and was glad I had the chance to see it. I wanted to walk to Lumbini but met with a lot of negativity from people. They told me all the terrible things that might happen – I might starve, or get lost, or be robbed or killed, and it was too cold to sleep out at nights. Although it's easy to travel from place to place by bus with the pilgrims, and they're quite willing to take you, I wouldn't have enjoyed that at all. Originally, I was not going to use roads at all and go cross-country from village to village, but this proved impracticable. Fifteen years ago when I was here, the paddy fields were empty all winter, but now they're full of crops: winter wheat, rape, tapioca, sugar cane, vegetables. And here in Nepal they're still harvesting the rice in some places.

Anyway, in spite of other people's negativity, I thought I should at least give walking a try. So I thought of all the *good* things that might happen, the kind, helpful people I might meet, etc., and decided to walk to Lumbini.

On my first attempt at *pindapata* [almsround] in Bulrampur, I did quite well – not a square meal, but enough to keep me going. One problem was trying to explain to people that I didn't accept money or raw rice. Also I think perhaps some people thought I was broke – a hard-up hippie. So then I got a monk to write a note (in Hindi) saying something like, 'I am a Buddhist monk on pilgrimage to the holy places. I do not accept money. I depend on almsfood and eat only between dawn and midday. I am grateful for your help.' With this note things have been easier. I stand in front of a shop or house for a while – maybe half a minute – and if they don't say anything, I move on to the next. If they ask what I want, then I give them the note to read. In most cases the response has been very good. Sometimes someone will walk along with me and chivvy their friends into giving me something. I usually look like the pied piper with a great gaggle of ragged children on my tail. One day I had quite a good meal of chapatis and sabjees and sweets. Other times I had small bits and pieces.

I've slept in a variety of places; by the road in a small copse of trees with a stream running through it (plenty of streams in this area, so no problem bathing); one night in a straw stack. The villagers wanted me to sleep in a house in the village, but there were too many women and children around, so I slept outside the village in the threshing area on a heap of straw, under a large mango tree. That was one of the warmest nights. Sleeping out is very cold and it is usually impossible to sleep lying down. But I remembered my experiences in Kanchanaburi [in Thailand], and found that I could make more economical use of my robes, and keep warmer by sitting up. One night I found an abandoned grass hut near the road. Daytime is pleasantly warm, but it gets a bit hot in the sun around midday, if you're walking or exerting yourself.

I regret I can't speak the language. I think it would be even more fruitful if I could. I've decided to carry on the rest of the pilgrimage in this way, going next to Kushinara, then Varanasi and Bodh Gaya. Of course, some of the dangers that people have pointed out might happen, but I'm sure they were just as likely in the Buddha's day, and I could probably more easily be killed by a taxi in London than by robbers in India.

I'm sure that my greatest protection is keeping the Vinaya-discipline. The *parami* [virtue] of keeping good Vinaya is very powerful; especially important are rules about food and money. If I kept food or money, I could not go *pindapata* with a clear conscience. Many people have done their best to persuade me to accept money or carry food with me, but I know if I did that then *pindapata* wouldn't work, I would not get any of the help or respect that usually go to a *samana* [renunciant].

I'm now in Lumbini. I stopped at Kapilavastu for one day, but there's not much to see. It doesn't appear to have been a very big place – nothing like Savatthi – but it's hard to say, as so little has been excavated. You can see the Himalayas from here. At Savatthi you couldn't see them. On the second day's walk I looked up in the late afternoon, and there they were; quite took my breath away. Green fields and trees stretching into the distance and beyond, the purple brown foothills, beyond this the snowcapped peaks against a vivid blue sky. The best time to see them is early morning, before eight; especially at sunrise, when the snow is bright pink. . . .

I had a lot of doubts about doing this while I was still in England. When I first arrived in India I had doubts too. Sometimes I thought I was completely crazy, or that it was just a waste of time, a distraction, or just ego. But now I'm very glad I'm able to do this trip. I consider myself very lucky to have the opportunity. I hope more monks will do the same. . . .

I hope all goes well with everyone at Chithurst. Excuse my terrible writing, but I'm not used to writing so small.

Metta,
Bodhipalo

VENERABLE AMARO

Venerable Amaro (Jeremy Horner) was born in Kent, England in 1956. He studied Psychology and Physiology at Bedford College, University of London. His first spiritual interest arose on reading the works of Rudolph Steiner. Upon completing his degree, he had the chance to travel to Asia – a friend offered him work as a groom on a cargo plane transporting racehorses to Malaysia.

He visited North-East Thailand on the recommendation of some people he met while travelling. Looking for a place to stay a few nights (before going on to Japan), he heard about Wat Pah Nanachat and its Western monks. The visit was eventful – he took an instant liking to the monks, felt immediately at home, and decided to stay. He became an anagarika, and then a samanera four months later (in 1978). The following year he received *upasampada* from Ajahn Chah.

Venerable Amaro stayed in Thailand for two years before family illness called him back to England. He then joined Ajahn Sumedho at the newly established Chithurst Monastery. Once while in London, he decided to look up a cousin of his whom he had never met: the illustrious scholar, translator and president of the Pali Text Society, I.B. Horner. Unfortunately, she died before a meeting between them could be arranged.

In 1983 Ajahn Sumedho asked him to take up residence at Harnham Vihara, and he requested (and was given permission) to make his way there on foot. He wrote a book about the 830-mile walk: *Tudong – the Long Road North,* in 1984.

No Empty Ideal

This talk was given by the Venerable Amaro during a retreat conducted for lay people at Amaravati Buddhist Centre in April 1986.

**What 'Buddha' means in our lives is more important
than whether the Buddha Gotama actually lived,
taught and did all the things he is said to have done.**

BEING ON A RETREAT LIKE THIS, a great sense of fellowship develops: a sense of everybody being on the same journey. Even though we come from an enormous variety of backgrounds, men and women, young and old, we are all heading for the same place. This is something we know in our hearts is true – that even though we may have different names for the goal of the spiritual life, something in us knows we are all heading in the same direction.

The most important thing about religious practice of any sort is that it is to be a process of awakening; it must not get trapped into being an empty ideal that we worship, instead of being a reality we open to. Many rivers of blood have been shed arguing about different names for the goal: 'The Holy City', 'Union with Brahma', 'Kismet', 'Nibbana'. As long as there have been people there have been ways of symbolizing the state of peace, security and fulfilment. So, if we can avoid getting caught up with the wording of the signpost – ending up hanging onto the signpost itself – as long as there is the resolution to make the journey, we will arrive, regardless of the name of the destination we have used.

How could the goals be different? Whether one is brought up a Christian, a Hindu or a Jew, as an English or an Asian person, how could the fundamental nature of the mind be different? How could it possibly be affected just by what we believe? Just as the nature of water is not affected by the shape of the vessel into which it is poured, so too the nature of Ultimate Truth – the nationality and the conditioning of the person in whom it is realized does not affect the way it actually is.

It is very important to remain determined to make the journey, to follow the signposts to awakening. The Buddha was extremely careful in the way he taught, to account for the human tendency to wander off the path. Our minds are so active and bright that we will always find some fascinating things to get involved in along the way: interesting places to visit, plants to investigate, people to chat with by the road. So he kept pointing out to people the crucial need to make the journey, rather than to just talk or think about it.

Around any religious teaching, over the years, there seems to grow up an enormous quantity of metaphysical and philosophical ideas; rites and rituals; traditions of what to eat, how to arrange marriages and funerals; how to talk about the different qualities of our minds and the different factors that influence our lives. Although we might start off with basic symbols to represent simple truths, in time they become things we worship in themselves. The institution becomes more important than the people who comprise it, and it is forgotten what the institution, and the symbol, were actually for. We end up worshipping the signpost rather than allowing it to point out the way to us.

To avoid this the Buddha kept his teaching very simple. One day he was walking through a forest with his monks; he picked up a handful of leaves and said: 'What do you think, bhikkhus, are there more leaves in my hand or more leaves in the forest?' 'The leaves in your hand are few and the leaves in the forest are many,' they replied. 'So too,' said the Buddha, 'the things that I know are comparable to the leaves in the forest, but that which I teach you is just as much as I hold in my hand.'

All the Buddha knew in terms of how the world works, the history of the universe, the astral realms, the mechanics of nature in all its multifaceted complexity – all this he laid aside. He kept his teaching simply to that which was crucial to liberation.

Because of this he refrained from getting into any kind of metaphysical discussion; he would never engage in that. Whenever anyone would try to draw him on such a point – 'What was the

Ultimate beginning?', 'What happens to an enlightened being when he dies?' – he would remain silent. He simply would not pursue it. Firstly, because these things are all unimportant, in that they do not lead directly to liberation; and secondly, to avoid compounding the wrong views of the questioner. He used a very good simile to explain this once: 'If I had a fire and put it out, and then I asked you: "Where has the fire gone – north, south, east or west?", what would you answer?' 'Well, it's a foolish question, because those things do not apply. It's just gone out, it hasn't gone anywhere.' The Buddha replied: 'Exactly so – the way you phrase the question assumes a particular kind of answer. So to give any answer is to go along with your mistaken view.'

So he would only teach that which related directly to what a person can do in order to realize the Truth. Whenever he did talk about Ultimate Reality, he would use the most impersonal and open terms: 'It is wonderful; immanent, peaceful; the Unoriginated, Unconditioned' – which do not give a great deal to grab a hold of! It is not some 'thing' one can externalize and idealize, but a quality one can open to and realize.

The essence of all spiritual practice, in our human condition, is to learn to look beyond the sensory world, learn to abide beyond perception. One way that we can do this is to look upon life as something that flows through the mind. Rather than thinking of oneself as a person who is going places, consider these as images going through the mind. Right now we have the image of the meditation hall, Amaravati; this is what we can perceive. The sound of this voice; the feeling of sitting on a cushion; the sense of sight; see that all these things flow through the mind like a current. When Ajahn Sumedho went travelling recently he said he made the determination before he left that he wasn't going to go around the world, he was just going to let the world go through his mind. Afterwards he said the result was very peaceful: he went everywhere, saw everyone, did everything, but the sense of movement, of a person heading towards somewhere, was absent; there was stillness in its place.

If we stop looking upon our sensory experience as being so solid and absolute, we see that there are just these perceptions, and the knowing – the sense of awareness and being. This is the way that the mind is liberated, the way beyond birth and death. There was a woman staying here in January who had terminal cancer, she came to die here as a nun. This was during a monastic retreat period so we had a lot of opportunity to contemplate the dying process. One afternoon, as I was doing some walking meditation, it struck me very clearly that when you look upon your life as a succession of images that the mind is aware of, then why should that be broken by the moment of death? The body is something that is perceived in the mind so, at the moment of death, if there has been awareness of the body alive, then surely there will just be awareness of the body dead. The body dies – just another perception in the mind. What that mind is attached to, where it goes, who it belongs to – are all the north, south, east and west of the matter. They are questions which do not really apply.

This is being with the mind that is beyond birth and death – being that knowing, being Buddha. When you see a thought arising in your mind, it appears, has its lifespan, and then it's gone. Though the birth and death of the body are probably the most powerful experiences we have in a human life, fundamentally there is no difference between them and the perception of a thought. With meditation practice there is the development of understanding how things come out of the void and go back into the void again. The more familiar we get with this process, the more the mysteries of existence resolve themselves. So it's not as though you know the answer, in so many words, to, 'Where do I come from, where do I go?', but you don't need to put it into words. You know the mind out of which everything arises and into which everything disappears.

By training yourself to just *be* that knowing, be that which is the source and goal of all things, you see the fear of the unknown dissolve. Death is frightening when we don't understand; but the more one knows the mind, the more it's no longer the unknown. There is no more fear because you realize, with the death of the body, what is there fundamentally different that could happen?

How could it not just be another thing that comes into the mind, that we bear with and then see vanish? Since we know the mind before and after things have been born into it, we know there is nothing to be frightened of.

In order to be able to deal with life this way we have to develop an undiscriminating attitude, welcoming everything that we experience. Welcoming the pleasant is very easy; pleasure is what we like. But there are unpleasant qualities that keep arising too: feelings of irritation and pride, desire, one's inability to be a perfect human being – welcoming all of that is a different story, isn't it?

I remember talking with Ajahn Sumedho one day about the practice of loving-kindness. 'It's those foolish and petty, childish emotional reactions I find hard to deal with.' 'Right,' he replied, 'but notice the way we describe them – "petty", "foolish", "childish" – does that sound to you like *metta*? Does that set things up for you to accept life wholeheartedly? Or does it show that you have already prejudged the whole experience? Because that's what I used to do. You have to welcome it all sincerely.'

As I began to apply this advice I realized how much of my time had been trying to fend off all those little imps and demons. All those wavelets of desire, fear and discomfort; subtle feelings that had never been very clear. Every time anything arose which brought a dismissive reaction up in my mind, I would say, very carefully and deliberately: 'Oh, jealousy, how nice of you to come! Have a seat. Pride! Hello... cup of tea?' The effect on my mind was astonishing. I realized how much of a problem I had been making out of my life – so much judging and choosing over what I wanted to arise in my thoughts.

I realized also that every time I reacted negatively, pushing things away, that action implied that there was something to fear. That this feeling or this thought was dangerous; that it was going to really hurt me, or invade me; that it was something that was really me and mine. As I began to welcome it all I realized that when you accept everything, only then can you sense that, after all, there is nothing to fear. None of it really belongs to a self or comes from a self. It cannot touch the mind which knows, cannot affect its nature. Whatever shape of vessel you pour the water into, with this same total accommodation, the water changes to the shape of the bottle. It doesn't say: 'I will not be poured into a square bottle, square bottles are not my scene. Round bottles only, please!' To push away or grasp a hold of the beautiful and the ugly, the noble and the sordid, is just as absurd really, isn't it?

When there is complete acceptance, there is just the sense of being the knowing, being that which is aware of all that comes through the mind. This is what the image of the Buddha at the moment of enlightenment symbolizes – one often sees pictures of the Buddha sitting under the Bodhi tree, with an aura of light around him. Very still. Awake. And all about him there is every kind of alluring, terrifying, heart-rending form imaginable – the hordes of Mara. Despite all his efforts, however, Mara fails to move the Buddha, and this is the moment of the Buddha's enlightenment. He knew: the beautiful, the terrifying, the sense of duty – all of these were just images in the mind. There is nothing one can grasp, there is nothing to fear, none of it can really touch the mind.

Now this is a symbol, and whether or not the incident occurred exactly as it is described is not as important as what it symbolizes. For one who practises the teaching, what 'Buddha' means in our lives is more important than whether the Buddha Gotama actually lived, taught and did all the things he is said to have done. 'Buddha' is that awakened nature of the mind, the heart of the mind. That in you which is wise, which knows, which is clear and bright. And that is what the Buddha on the night of his enlightenment represents – that knowing.

All the hordes of Mara – these are just the thoughts and feelings, hopes and fears, memories, pleasures and pains of daily activity. These may not be as grand as the alluring daughters, the terrifying demons or the tears of old King Suddhodana – getting the children to school, trying to please the boss, brushing your teeth – but for us these are the hordes of Mara. The images of daily life come pouring through the mind but, if we are awake, we can see that none of it affects the mind's true nature – that sense of stillness, knowing, spaciousness and clarity which the Buddha represents.

Most of the time, however, we find ourselves moving away from that point. That's our habitual reaction to the world – grasping after things or running away from things. I remember, when I was a very small child, often trying to jump into the middle of my shadow, but however hard I jumped I just landed on the shadow's feet. And I would run after my shadow and then jump – but where would I land up? Just in the same place all over again. And this is what we do with our lives – the things that we desire, it's like running after shadows. You try to catch hold, reaching for the desire so close, so close, and then you grasp it and then... and you haven't *really* got it. Somehow it's not what you expected, it's different, not what you really wanted.

And then to run from your shadow – to be afraid, you keep turning around: 'It's still behind me, run faster, got to get away.' When we stop and look though, we realize: 'Well, it's just my shadow.' You can't get away from it, but there's nothing in it to be afraid of, it's just a shadow.

So when we stop and rest in the stillness of knowing, we know in our hearts that all we desire, all we fear, are just shadows. There is no substance there – nothing which can make us more complete and nothing which can threaten us. This is the real freedom of mind.

So being Buddha, being that still, aware, noble being, is both the goal and the practice that we follow – the goal of the practice and the substance of the practice are the same. The religious path is thus one of simply learning to rest in being that Knowing, being Buddha, awake and aware.

VENERABLE THANAVARO

Venerable Thanavaro (Giuseppe Proscia) was born in the north-east of Italy in 1955. Having shown a keen interest in the arts from an early age, he studied music, dance and drama. Conscripted into the Italian army, he met a disciple of a Tibetan lama, who introduced him to Buddhism. After serving his year's national service, he spent a while in London studying music, and worked in a fast-food restaurant. Some time later, back in Italy, he read (in a Christmas Humphreys book) about Buddhist centres in England, and in a casual conversation in a cafe heard about Ajahn Sumedho. Returning to England, he went to meet Ajahn Sumedho at the Oakenholt Buddhist Centre near Oxford, where the monks were temporarily residing.

In October 1977, he became an anagarika at the Hampstead Vihara, and a samanera one year later. He received *upasampada* in 1979 on a boat on the River Thames, his preceptor being Venerable Dr. Saddhatissa. Thus he was the first Western monk training in Ajahn Chah's monasteries to be ordained in England.

Venerable Thanavaro spent six years at Chithurst Monastery and Harnham Vihara, before accompanying Venerable Viradhammo to New Zealand in 1985, to help establish a vihara in Wellington.

GENERATING BLESSINGS

The following teaching by Venerable Thanavaro has been taken from a response to a question asked at a public talk in Palmerston North, New Zealand, 1988. The classic Buddhist text being commented upon is known as the Mahamangala Sutta – 'The Discourse on Great Blessings' – from the Sutta Nipata.

Because the truth is 'inside' and not just 'outside', it is a source of blessings.

MEDITATION IS THAT WHICH ENABLES US TO BE AWARE of the process of change. And this process of change is the process of life. If we're not able to acknowledge this process then we resist it. We act in habitual ways and lose our spontaneity. We pile up all kinds of problems in our minds.

It would be nice if in the morning when we wash our face we could give a good scrub to our mind also – you know, somehow everything that was worrying us was left behind – we could come out feeling really fresh and new! But it doesn't work like that, does it?

However, there is a way that does cleanse the mind. It is the way of bringing blessings into our life. Now do you know how to bring blessings into your life? I'm sure most of us have tried to do this. Some people try to bring blessings into their lives by bringing more money into their pockets, but money is not necessarily always a blessing. The blessings that I am talking about are blessings that come through understanding; they are brought about by right motivation. Whenever we have right motivation we bring blessings into our life – we bring happiness into our life.

So first of all – 'to associate with good friends and not be caught up with foolish people' – that is a way of bringing blessings into our life. The company of the wise is a source of blessings. Also, the way we relate to those good and wise friends brings blessings. Whenever our heart is humble, and we are able to give homage, that very attitude is a source of blessing.

'To live in a good place' – that means a place which is conducive to peacefulness and calm – is a source of blessings. For example, living in the centre of New York City doesn't exactly facilitate a cascade of blessings into your life.

'Taking care of our parents, our children, our partner, and friends' is a source of blessings. 'To have a skill' and 'to work with others without conflict' is a source of blessings.

'To listen continuously' and therefore be attentive is a source of blessings. Through listening and being attentive we recognize the truth of what is being said – the truth is awakened 'within' us. Because the truth is 'inside' and not just 'outside', it is a source of blessings. And 'discussion on the truth' – sharing of one's experiences – is a source of blessings. This is not the sharing of gossip about each other, that's *not* a source of blessings – but this is a sharing in the light of giving.

[*To the audience*] Do you know of any other source of blessings – anything else that brings happiness into your life?

Meditation . . . contentment . . . gratitude . . . giving . . . giving of oneself . . . .

So, yes! Meditation and the ability to clear the mind: are you all familiar with this skill? If the mind is not clear then it is obstructed, isn't it? And whenever the mind is obstructed we experience problems. One after another they pile up. Since the mind in its true nature is like empty space, we can stack all the problems in until there's a nervous breakdown. That means you've had enough! A nervous breakdown is a way of releasing the accumulated dirt of the mind – all the daily irritations and frustrations.

My teacher, Ajahn Sumedho, describes meditation as a kind of 'controlled nervous breakdown'. That means that you are in control, you are the master, observing this process of gradual release. And all sorts of stuff will come up, you know. I won't tell you some of the things that have come up in my mind.

In Buddhism we say that before the mind is restored to its pristine awareness it is obstructed by three poisons. The three poisons that continually contaminate the stream of consciousness are greed or lust, aversion – which culminates in hatred – and stupidity. And they say you can have eighty-four thousand variations on this theme of greed, hatred and stupidity. So you can really be creative!

Now you know some people are striving to transcend these tendencies. Transcending these tendencies is the process of meditation – the process that liberates us. Any questions about this?

VENERABLE JAYASARO

Venerable Jayasaro (Shaun Chiverton) was born on the Isle of Wight, England, in 1958. At school he excelled academically, but a spell of three weeks in Morocco with the Venture Scouts when he was 14 had whetted his appetite for travel, and when he left school he decided to go overland by bus to India.

For the next 18 months he travelled extensively throughout India, acquiring an interest in Eastern religion and meditation practice along the way. Hitch-hiking back in 1977, he spent three months in Iran teaching English. Declining the offer of a place at Sussex University, he went to work for his father who was an engineer.

During the following year he started visiting the Hampstead Vihara, and in 1978 he became an anagarika, spending the *vassa* with Ajahn Sumedho at Oakenholt, near Oxford. He then went to Thailand with the intention of becoming a bhikkhu, and he received *upasampada* from Ajahn Chah in 1980. Currently he lives at Wat Pah Nanachat, where he assists with the training of monks. In 1988, he accompanied Tan Chao Khun Paññananda on a visit to England.

LUANG POR'S WAY

*In 1986 Venerable Jayasaro, along with Venerable Abhichat, was
asked by the senior monks of Wat Pah Pong to prepare Ajahn Chah's
biography. In 1988 the former visited the U.K. as a translator for
Venerable Chao Khun Paññananda – also to spend time with his family.
The following reflections on Ajahn Chah's life are taken from a talk
given at Amaravati Buddhist Centre in June of that year.*

**In later times when Ajahn Chah had disciples,
he excelled in skilful means for helping them;
he had had so many problems himself.**

MY OWN FIRST MEETING WITH AJAHN CHAH was on the
full moon of December 1978. I had spent the 'Rains' retreat of
that year as an eight-precept lay person with Ajahn Sumedho
at Oakenholt here in England. After the retreat I went out to
Thailand. When I arrived at Wat Pah Pong, Venerable Pamutto,
an Australian monk resident there at the time, took me to see
Ajahn Chah. He was sitting under his *kuti* having a drink. He
looked at me and smiled very warmly. He held out the drink he
had in his hand so I crawled over and took it. As I returned to
my place I found there were tears welling up in my eyes. I was
emotionally overcome for quite a while. Since that day I don't
think I have ever wanted to leave the monastery or do anything
except be a disciple of Ajahn Chah.

People often presumed there would be a problem with language for
Westerners who wanted to stay at the monastery, but this was not
the case. Someone once asked Ajahn Chah: 'Luang Por, how do
you teach all your Western disciples? Do you speak English or
French? Do you speak Japanese or German?'

'No,' replied Ajahn Chah.

'Then how do they all manage?' he asked.

'Householder,' Ajahn Chah enquired, 'at your home do you have
water-buffaloes?' 'Yes Luang Por,' was the reply.

'Do you have any cows, or dogs, or chickens?' 'Yes Luang Por.'

'Tell me,' Luang Por asked, 'do you speak water-buffalo; do you speak cow?' 'No,' the householder replied.

'Well, how do they all manage?'

Language was not so important to Luang Por. He knew how to see through the exterior trappings of language and culture. He could see how basically all minds revolve around the same old centres of greed, hatred and delusion. His method of training was one of pointing directly at the way our minds work. He was always showing us how craving gives rise to suffering – actually allowing us to see *directly* the Four Noble Truths. And for him, the way of exposing desires was to frustrate them. In his vocabulary, the words 'to teach' and 'to torment' were more or less interchangeable.

Such training as this can only take place if everyone in the monastery has great confidence in the teacher. If there is the slightest suspicion that he might be doing it out of aversion, or desire for power, then there wouldn't be any benefit. In Ajahn Chah's case everyone could see that he had the greatest courage and fortitude and so could trust that he was doing it out of compassion.

Primarily he would teach about letting go. But he also taught a lot about what to do when we can't let go. 'We endure,' he would say. Usually people could appreciate *intellectually* all about letting go, but when faced with obstacles they couldn't do it. The teaching of patient endurance was a central aspect of the way that he taught. He continually changed routines around in the monastery so you wouldn't become stuck in ruts. As a result you kept finding yourself not quite knowing where you stood. And he would always be there watching so you couldn't be too heedless. This is one of the great values of living with a teacher; one *feels* the need to be mindful.

In looking into Ajahn Chah's early life it was inspiring for me to find just how many problems he had. Biographies of some great masters leave you with the impression that the monks were perfectly pure from the age of eight or nine – that they didn't have to work at their practice. But for Ajahn Chah practice was very difficult; for one thing he had a lot of sensual desire. He also had a great deal of desire for beautiful requisites – bowl and robes, etc. He made a resolution in working with these tendencies that he would never ask for anything – even if it was permitted to do so by the Discipline. He related once how his robes had been falling to bits; his under-robe was worn paper-thin so he had to walk very carefully, lest it split. Then one day he heedlessly squatted down and it tore completely. He didn't have any cloth to patch it but remembered the foot-wiping cloths in the Meeting Hall. So he took them away, washed them and patched his robe with them.

In later times when he had disciples, he excelled in skilful means for helping them; he had had so many problems himself. In another story, he related how he made a resolution to really work with sensual desire. He resolved that for the three-month 'Rains' retreat he would not look at a woman. Being very strong-willed, he was able to keep to it. On the last day of the retreat many people came to the monastery to make offerings. He thought: 'I've done it now for three months, let's see what happens.' He looked up and at that moment there was a young woman right in front of him. He said the impact was like being hit by lightning. It was then that he realized mere sense restraint, although essential, was not enough. No matter how restrained one may be regarding the eyes, ears, nose, tongue, body, and mind, if there wasn't wisdom to understand the actual nature of desire, then freedom from it was impossible.

He was always stressing the importance of wisdom: not just restraint, but mindfulness and contemplation. Throwing oneself into practice with great gusto and little reflective ability may result in a strong concentration practice, but eventually one ends up in despair. Monks practising like this usually come to a point where they decide that they don't have what it takes to 'break through' in this lifetime, and disrobe. He emphasized that continuous effort was much more important than making a great effort for a short while – only to let it all slide. Day in, day out; month in, month out; year, in year out: that is the real skill of the practice.

What is needed in mindfulness practice, he taught, is a *constant* awareness of what one is thinking, doing or saying. It is not a matter of being on retreat or off retreat, or of being in a monastery or out wandering on *tudong*; it's a matter of constancy. '*What* am I doing now; *why* am I doing it?' – constantly looking to see what is happening in the present moment. 'Is this mind-state coarse or refined?' In the beginning of practice, he said, our mindfulness is intermittent like water dripping from a tap. But as we continue, the intervals between the drips lessen and eventually they become a stream. This stream of mindfulness is what we are aiming for.

It was noticeable that he did not talk a lot about levels of enlightenment or various states of concentration absorption (*jhana*). He was aware of how people tend to attach to these terms and conceive of practice as going from this stage to that. Once someone asked him if such and such a person was an *arahant* – was enlightened. He answered: 'If they are then they are, if they're not then they're not; you are what you are, and you're not like them. So just do your own practice.' He was very short with such questions.

When people asked him about his own attainments, he never spoke praising himself or making any claim whatsoever. When talking about the foolishness of people, he wouldn't say: '*You* think like this and *you* think like that,' or '*You* do this and *you* do that.' Rather, he would always say: '*We* do this and *we* do that.' The skill of speaking in such a personal manner meant those listening regularly came away feeling that he was talking directly to them. Also, it often happened that people would come with personal problems they wanted to discuss with him, and that very same evening he would give a talk covering exactly that subject.

In setting up his monasteries, he took a lot of his ideas from the great meditation teacher Venerable Ajahn Mun, but also from other places he encountered during his years of wandering. Always he laid great emphasis on a sense of community. In one section of the *Mahaparinibbana Sutta* ['Dialogues of the Buddha,' Sutta 16] the Buddha speaks about the welfare of the Sangha being dependent on meeting frequently in large numbers, in harmony, and on discussing things together. Ajahn Chah stressed this a lot.

The Bhikkhu-Discipline – *Vinaya* – was to Ajahn Chah a very important tool for training. He had found it so in his own practice. Often he would give talks on it until one or two o'clock in the morning; the bell would then ring at three for morning chanting. Monks were sometimes afraid to go back to their *kutis* lest they couldn't wake up, so they would just lean against a tree.

Especially in the early days of his teaching things were very difficult. Even basic requisites like lanterns and torches were rare. In those days the forest was dark and thick with many wild and dangerous animals. Late at night you could hear the monks going back to their huts making a loud noise, stomping and chanting at the same time. On one occasion, twenty torches were given to the monastery. But as soon as the batteries ran out, they all came back into the stores as there weren't new batteries to replace them.

Sometimes Ajahn Chah was very harsh on those who lived with him. He admitted himself that he had an advantage over his disciples. He said that when his mind entered *samadhi*-concentration for only thirty minutes it could be the same as having slept all night. Sometimes he talked for literally hours. Going over and over the same things again and again, telling the same story hundreds of times. For him, each time was as if the first. He would be sitting there giggling and chuckling away and everybody else would be looking at the clock and wondering when he would let them go back.

It seemed that he had a special soft spot for those who suffered a lot; this often meant the Western monks. There was one English monk, Venerable Thitappo, whom he gave a lot of attention to; that means he tormented him terribly. One day there was a large gathering of visitors to the monastery and, as often happened, Ajahn Chah was praising the Western monks to the Thais as a way of teaching them. He was saying how clever the Westerners were, all the things they could do and what good disciples they were. 'All,' he said 'except this one,' pointing to Venerable Thitappo. 'He's really stupid.' Another day he asked Venerable Thitappo: 'Do you get angry when I treat you like this?' Venerable Thitappo replied: 'What use would it be? It would be like getting angry at a mountain.'

Several times people suggested to Ajahn Chah that he was like a Zen Master. 'No I'm not,' he would say, 'I'm like Ajahn Chah.' There was a Korean monk visiting once who liked to ask him *koans*. Ajahn Chah was completely baffled; he thought they were jokes. You could see how it was necessary to know the rules of the game before you could give the right answers. One day this monk told Ajahn Chah the Zen story about the flag and the wind and asked: 'Is it the flag that blows or is it the wind?' Ajahn Chah answered: 'It's neither; it's the mind'. The Korean monk thought that was wonderful and immediately bowed to Ajahn Chah. But then Ajahn Chah said he'd just read the story in the Thai translation of Hui Neng.

Many of us tend to confuse profundity with complexity, so Ajahn Chah liked to show how profundity was in fact simplicity. The truth of impermanence is the most simple thing in the world, and yet it is the most profound. He really emphasized that. He said the key to living in the world with wisdom is a regular recollection of the changing nature of things. 'Nothing is sure,' he would constantly remind us. He was always using this word in Thai – '*Mai-naa!*' – meaning 'uncertain'. This teaching: 'It's not certain,' he said, sums up all the wisdom of Buddhism. In meditation, he emphasized, 'We can't go beyond the hindrances unless we really understand them.' This means *knowing* their impermanence.

Often he talked about 'killing the defilements', and this also meant 'seeing their impermanence'. 'Killing defilements' is an idiomatic expression in the meditative Forest Tradition of North-East Thailand. It means that by seeing with penetrative clarity the actual nature of defilements, you go beyond them.

Whilst it was considered the 'job' of a bhikkhu in this tradition to be dedicated to formal practice, it didn't mean there wasn't work to do. When work needed doing you did it. And you didn't make a fuss. Work is not any different from formal practice if one knows the principles properly. The same principles apply in both cases, as it's the same body and mind.

And in Ajahn Chah's monasteries, when the monks worked, they *really* worked. One time he wanted a road built up to Wat Tum

Saeng Pet mountain monastery, and the Highways Department offered to help. But before long they pulled out. So Ajahn Chah took the monks up there to do it. Everybody worked from three o'clock in the afternoon until three o'clock the next morning. A rest was allowed until just after five when they would head off down the hill to the village on almsround. After the meal they could rest again until three, before starting work once more. But nobody saw Ajahn Chah take a rest; he was busy receiving people who came to visit. And when it was time to work, he didn't just direct it. He joined in the heavy lifting and carrying of rocks alongside everyone else. That was always very inspiring for the monks to see: hauling water from the well, sweeping and so on, he was always there – right up until the time his health began to fail.

Ajahn Chah wasn't always popular in his province in North-East Thailand, even though he did bring about many major changes in the lives of the people. There was a great deal of animism and superstition in their belief systems. Very few people practised meditation, out of fear that it would drive them crazy. There was more interest in magical powers and psychic phenomena than in Buddhism. A lot of killing of animals was done in the pursuit of merit. Ajahn Chah was often very outspoken on such issues, so at first he had many enemies.

Nevertheless, there were always many who loved him. And it was clear that he never played on that. In fact, if any of his disciples were getting too close, he would send them away. Sometimes monks became attached to him, and he promptly sent them off to some other monastery. As charismatic as he was, he always stressed the importance of Sangha – of community spirit.

One New Year's Eve I remember how, in accordance with custom, a vast number of people had come to the monastery. After the evening chanting Ajahn Chah gave a talk, and this was followed by meditation. Just before midnight someone came in and announced that a senior monk from the village monastery had arrived. I remember how Ajahn Chah went out and received the monk himself: came in carrying his bag and proceeded to lay out his sitting-cloth. He then made the three most beautiful bows of respect that I have ever seen. In every way he displayed heartfelt humility: as if he were a monk just newly ordained. In the middle of many hundreds of his disciples it was as though he were completely immune to all the unskilful feelings that many of us may have felt.

I think it was because Ajahn Chah was 'nobody in particular' that he could be anybody he chose. If he felt it was necessary to be fierce, he could be that. If he felt that somebody would benefit from warmth and kindness, then he would give that. You had the feeling he would be whatever was helpful for the person he was with. And he was very clear about the proper understanding of conventions. Someone once asked him about the relative merits of *arahants* and *bodhisattvas*. He answered: 'Don't be an *arahant*, don't be a *bodhisattva,* don't be anything at all. If you are an *arahant* you will suffer, if you are *bodhisattva* you will suffer, if you are anything at all you will suffer.' I had the feeling that Ajahn Chah wasn't anything at all. The quality in him that one was inspired by was the light of Dhamma he reflected; it wasn't exactly him as a person.

So since first meeting Ajahn Chah, I have had an unshakable conviction that this way is truly possible – it works – it is good enough. And I've found a willingness to acknowledge that, if there are any problems, it's me who is creating them. It's not the form and it's not the teachings. This appreciation has made things a lot easier.

It's important that we are able to learn from all the ups and downs we have in practice. It's important that we come to know how to be 'a refuge unto ourselves' – to see clearly for ourselves. When I consider the morass of selfishness and foolishness my life could have been. . . . And then reflecting on the teachings and benefits I've received, I find I really want to dedicate my life to being a credit to my teacher. Such reflection has been a great source of strength. This is one form of *sanghanusati* – 'Recollection on Sangha' – recollection of the great debt we owe our teachers.

So I trust that you may find this is of some help in your practice.

VENERABLE VAJIRO

Venerable Vajiro (Phil Gunton) was born in Kuala Lumpur, Malaysia, in 1953. He was educated at Lancing College in England, and went on to study Economics at Bath University. Upon graduating in 1974, he took up a career in accountancy. During this period, a friend encouraged him to go on a ten-day meditation retreat with John Coleman at the Oakenholt Buddhist Centre near Oxford. He attended further retreats there in 1976 and 1977.

Hearing about the visit Ajahn Chah and Ajahn Sumedho made to Oakenholt in 1977, he went to meet them at the Hampstead Vihara. He eventually moved next door to the vihara, while continuing his training as an accountant. In 1978, however, he asked to join the community as an anagarika; he then stayed a while at Chithurst, before travelling to Wat Pah Pong in Thailand. He became a samanera there in 1979, and received *upasampada* from Ajahn Chah the following year.

Venerable Vajiro returned to England in 1984, and assisted with the establishment of Amaravati Buddhist Centre. He presently resides at Chithurst Monastery.

DANA

The following teaching has been taken from a talk given by Venerable Vajiro at Chithurst Buddhist Monastery in 1988.

'Giving' is the beginning and the end
of the religious life.

THE FEELING OF SEPARATION is an experience that all living beings have. We come across it within ourselves and can see it in animals also. There's a recognition that 'this' is separate from 'that'; this body is separate from that one. And we make various attempts to get over this sense of separation. Perhaps the most primitive reaction to it, is 'taking'. We take from the environment around us – absorbing into ourself. We take food and we take power. This 'taking' can be one way of trying to cope with the sense of separation.

A slightly more refined way of trying to cope with this experience is 'making a bargain', one being with another – a sort of agreement. We give something to get something in return: 'If I give this much, then I expect that much back'. Using such bargaining structures is perhaps the most common way we relate with each other as humans – the shopping we do, agreements we make with our spouse, or with the children: 'I'll give you this and you give me that.' So this can be another way of dealing with this feeling of separateness.

Then there is sharing. That's a little bit more open, isn't it? There's a recognition of the separation of one being from an other, and a willingness to share. In this way both parties are benefitting from the arrangement. It's akin to a bargain, but it's a little more spacious, both expecting some sort of enjoyment from it – some sort of gratification.

But with each of these ways of relating, there's always reinforcement of the sense of separateness. With taking, with bargaining, and even with sharing there's still a sense of one being separate from the other. So it's not really transcending or getting beyond our separateness. This is where *dana* works so well. With dana or *real* giving, *real* generosity, there is no expectation of return. It's not a bargain, it's not even a sharing. It's not that we share something with another, and keep some for ourself. We actually give completely, without expecting anything back.

A lot of our giving is not giving completely. It's imperfect giving. But this is something that can be worked on. We can consider how to perfect giving over a period of time. It is the first of the 'Ten Paramitas'*. We understand from the texts that it was the last of the ten that the Buddha perfected, but as Theravadin Buddhists, we have it first on the list.

I think Ajahn Buddhadasa once said that if we perfect one of the paramitas fully, then all the others are perfected also. That's very helpful when considering dana. We can see how if we practise giving without expecting anything in return, all the paramitas can be fulfilled at that moment.

One has to use wisdom – *pañña* – to know for example, the right time and place and the right things to give. And to give honestly – *sacca* – requires that we look at our intention clearly. And patience – *khanti*: we must be patient in the act of giving, and with our limitations in learning to give. There's renunciation there too: we give something that we perceive as being 'ours'. And we have to use energy – *viriya*. Also, whenever we give, there's the chance that our offering could be rejected, so we must develop *metta* and *upekkha*. And we have to 'resolve' to do it; it requires a determination to give – this is developing *adhitthana*. Also, resolving to share the merit of the act of generosity – making a dedication.

Now how can we notice these qualities – giving, renunciation, honesty – the whole spectrum of perfections that can exist in that simple act of giving? How do we really work with giving? When I was first in Thailand, I remember that receiving generosity was not easy. As a strong young man, walking on almsround and

---

*The Ten *Paramitas* ['virtues' or 'perfections'] are: generosity, moral discipline, renunciation, wisdom, energy, honesty, determination, patience, loving-kindness, and equanimity.

having the old village people come running out to offer a little bit of rice, a piece of fruit, a couple of pieces of palm sugar or whatever. . . . At times I thought: 'What on earth have I done to deserve this? I should really be helping these old villagers.' And yet, for those people practising generosity, they felt it was a privilege. You know, they'd be more annoyed if we didn't come on almsround. They would be round at the monastery saying: 'Well, why didn't you come today? Are you ill or something?' or 'You haven't been doing your duty.' I remember talking to Ajahn Jagaro at the time about how I felt, and he said: 'You'll never really learn how to give until you learn to receive, and you'll never learn how to receive until you learn to give.'

There are two sides to giving; there's receiving also. The gratitude – the appreciation of the spirit of giving. That doesn't necessarily mean liking what is offered; but appreciating the loveliness of the act of generosity – the act of giving without expecting anything in return. The humbling quality which comes with this gratitude is very helpful in transcending the sense of separation. This helps in going beyond the feeling of selfishness, of being separate.

We can give in many ways, of course: give materially, food, shelter, medicine, clothing, money. . . . We can give time, encouragement, kindness, love. . . . And all of these can be bargained with, taken, shared, or given. But it's not the quantity, or the thing itself that's important. It's the attitude of not expecting anything in return or not making some sort of agreement about it. When we do give in this way, then we find that there's no disappointment, and there's no fear either. There's no conceit and no arrogance. There's just giving.

Eventually, we come to recognize the 'giving of attention' – giving attention to 'this' moment and not expecting anything from it. We say that in Buddhist practice, all you have to do is 'be mindful'. What this actually means is that that is *all* we are doing; mindfulness is *all* that is happening. We're not expecting something back. To expect a return would be striking a bargain; 'giving' would not be perfected, and the sense of separation would not be transcended.

Giving attention to the moment is what we can practise all the time. Giving attention to the breath, not expecting anything from the breath. Giving attention to the posture, to the movements of the body. Giving attention throughout our life is a way of practising generosity: not expecting anything in return, not bargaining, not taking anything, not even sharing, just giving. That giving doesn't indulge and doesn't repress. It doesn't seek anything or try to get rid of anything. With such generosity, with dana, we can see the possibility of the perfection of humanity.

Classifying these ways of relating into taking, bargaining, sharing and giving may not come directly from the scriptures, but I hope it is helpful in your practice. To me, 'giving' is the beginning and the end of the religious life.

EPILOGUE: TRUE FRIENDS

*This letter from Venerable Kittisaro was previously printed in the
Devon Vihara Newsletter, in September 1987.*

DEAR FRIENDS ON THE PATH,

Greetings. Though I've seen many of you this summer here at the
Vihara or away at one of the public talks I've given, I've not had
the opportunity for quite a while to write a letter to you all. I think
it's important that occasionally we reflect upon ourselves as a part
of a larger community of beings all united in our inclination to
Nibbana, peace. The transforming effect of a virtuous community
is the power of Sangha. Though literally the word can mean any
sort of group or gathering, its usage in Buddhist practice is quite
specific.

Sangha is one of the precious Triple Gems, one of the Three
Refuges to which Buddhists continually go in their skilful effort
to return and re-establish themselves on the Way, moment to
moment. I go to Buddha, I go to Dhamma, I go to Sangha.

What is this 'going to Sangha', *Sangham saranam gacchami,* and
what does it have to do with Nibbana? In its strictest sense,
Sangha refers to those beings who have had true insight and are
firmly established in Right View. This *Ariya Sangha,* or group of
Noble Ones, can be made up of men and women, ordained people
and laity, young and old beings alike. *Ariya Sangha* don't even
have to be 'Buddhists'! Members of this virtuous order are
dedicated to practice: practising goodness, practising straightly –
avoiding the extremes of sensory indulgence or repressive self-
mortification – practising direct insight into the way things are,
and endeavouring to master these great efforts so that thoughts,
speech, and actions are conditioned by wisdom rather than
ignorance.

The members of the *Ariya Sangha* have had insight into the
Four Noble Truths. They know the cessation of suffering, the
experience of true peace. Though they may still be fooled by

beguiling conditions of mind and body (except in the case of *arahants*, who are never fooled), they can return to the Path, re-establishing Right View from the perspective of knowing this moment as it is. They can begin again. Members of this Noble Sangha can 'let go'. This is wisdom.

Basically, the *Ariya Sangha* is that group of wise beings. Why then is the third refuge 'I go to the Sangha'? Because wise beings are alive, flesh and blood, here and now, living examples of the Way. Their earthiness and tangibility often touches our heart when Buddha-Dhamma seems remote and abstract. Sangha brings the Teachings to life.

We need not, though, be obsessed with designating 'who knows' and 'who doesn't', 'who's truly wise' and 'who isn't'. 'Will the REAL Sangha members please stand up!' Even if we do hear or think that he or she is attained, we still need to be able to deal with the doubt arising in our own mind. 'Does he really know?'

More importantly, however, we need to develop that inner sense of what is wholesome and what isn't, what rings true and what doesn't. This discernment will tell us whether to trust someone or not. We don't need to rely on some official stamp of ecclesiastic authority – 'He's a stream enterer,' 'She's fully realized,' 'He's a non-returner,' etc. In fact, if we are moved by such claims, then we tend to blindly follow others' opinions, and never get beyond doubt.

Though it's impractical to designate 'Who's Who', the principal importance of a wise being remains. If we know individuals who inspire us with their presence, their practice, their insight, their goodness, then we should make an effort to respect them, learn from them, support them. The Buddha praised the great blessing of seeking out the wise rather than the foolish as companions. This is not to say blindly follow them. But just beginning to sense what is wise and what is not is the birth of the reflective mind. Then, to raise up that goodness in our hearts through various actions, we begin to bring those Sangha qualities into conscious-ness. After all, from a wise being we hear the true teaching. From the ignorant beings in our lives (and in our own minds) we hear about ME and YOU, TIME, I MUST HAVE, I MUST GET RID OF, and all the other 84,000 assorted delusions of greed, hatred and self-conceit.

'I go for refuge to the Sangha' means I will seek out a wise friend. The Buddha teaches that the wise ones are 'worthy of gifts, worthy of hospitality, worthy of offerings, worthy of respect. They give occasion for incomparable goodness to arise in the world.' Sangha is a true refuge. Let's remember that.

Traditionally, Sangha refers to those ordained bhikkhus and bhikkhunis, who are giving their lives to the practice of the Way. But strictly speaking, the Noble Sangha is open to all beings who have had true insight. Having a robe and a shaven head is no guarantee whatsoever of wisdom and virtue. When the monastic life is lived sincerely and earnestly it is conducive to developing virtue, insight and true accomplishment. In fact, in any lifestyle how we practise determines whether Sangha is present – not our robe, sex, occupation, or religious title.

In a broader and quite practical sense, Sangha can and should include all beings inclining towards peace, virtue, wisdom and compassion. As opposed to the worldly stream carrying groups of beings into whirlpools of passion, dogmatic views and despair, the power of Sangha is that counter-current and flow of beings towards the oceanic calm of kindness, compassion, joy and serenity – *metta, karuna, mudita, upekkha*. Good friends are so important for reminding us when we go astray, for inspiring and encouraging us, empowering us to begin again.

These definitions of Sangha all focus on outer beings, wise teachers, virtuous friends. When there is doubt, wavering, confusion within, the outer manifestations of wisdom illumine the way. Friends and wise beings in our lives, however, are part of this mind, our mind. Our worldly habits say HE and SHE OUT THERE, but really those beings are arising in our own minds, just as do our thoughts – and the thoughts of reading this letter as well. The qualities of wisdom and virtue that we recognize in others are also part of this mind that we call our own. Eventually we must realize that Sangha is essentially the boundless virtue within.

Our refuge in Sangha, our contact with wise beings, keeps directing our hearts to seeing the Buddha within, that in us which knows, which is aware now, which is not deluded by our experience. Our contact with Sangha reminds us, encourages us, in effect offers us occasions conducive to using this Buddha Nature within so the Dhamma is revealed, so that Truth – How Things Are – becomes clear in our minds. Our contact with Sangha outside, as manifested in our wise friends and virtuous companions, reminds us to cultivate these very same qualities unshakably within our hearts. True Sangha does not point to itself – 'We are the special ones' – but rather it points to the virtuous heart, to that skilful effort which brings us back again and again to practise the Dhamma.

This summer I've had the good fortune to experience the power of Sangha in many ways: leading retreats; participating in discussion groups; attending an ordination ceremony with fellow monks and nuns, and our teacher Venerable Sumedho; and learning from other spiritually-oriented groups. In the most ordinary and immediate sense, I live with monks and anagarikas who are dedicated to developing the Way. We are supported by our many generous friends. This humbles us, for we know that as alms mendicants we cannot live alone, and yet it inspires and warms our hearts to receive. Those conditions then generate a new round of Sangha virtue as we naturally feel motivated to make ourselves worthy of offerings, to practise well, to offer what we can.

Sangha generates Sangha generates Sangha: swelling spheres of goodness that meet and merge, leaving only joy and gratitude, the sense of inner and outer melted into one mind. These moments disappear when the overlapping spheres shrink down, the contracting power of identifying with ME and MINE collapsing space into independent alienated bubbles of being this or that. Trapped in our own private worlds, space is further splintered and fragmented into a maze of jagged beings, caught in a current of time, competing with one another for happiness. Life becomes very complicated and anxious, as we feel compelled to protect our fragile niche, or improve it, or take over someone else's. I think we have all felt like that.

Now remember how you felt when you encountered Sangha, a wise being, one who is at ease. When we hear the Truth or see it, or feel its peaceful manifestation, we can relax. Faith and trust are born. Suddenly, miraculously, the myriad divided beings begin to awaken to the truth of this moment; and where there was separation, a unifying universality begins to pervade our heart as we come together in attentiveness, wise reflection, virtuous effort. The differences are still apparent, but they do not divide us, for we stand together inspired by the Way itself. Many times I've seen this miracle happen and then dissolve. Coming together often with our dhamma friends helps to generate and sustain this 'right seeing' and dissolve that habitual tendency to contract our spacious heart into rigid self views.

Obviously, in our normal lives we will encounter many not-so-wise beings within and without. Learning to cope in this world with its many faces is painful and difficult, but with our refuge in Sangha we learn to find joy in Right Effort, no matter who's around. Then Sangha is established in our hearts, and all beings are our family, giving us precious teachings. *Sangham saranam gacchami* takes us home to the wise and virtuous one within. The virtuous ones 'without' remind us of the Way, and in gratitude we honour them and remember our true home: One Heart, One Knowing.

May all beings find a good friend.

Yours,
Kittisaro Bhikkhu

Thailand, 1969

Thailand, 1975

Thailand, 1975
Thailand, 1976

England, 1979

U.S.A., 1979

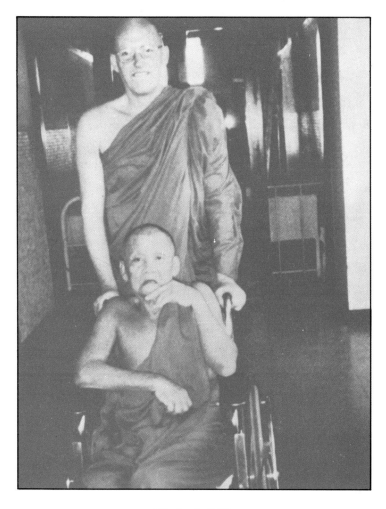

Thailand, 1982

GLOSSARY OF FOREIGN WORDS

The following words are mostly in Pali, the language of the Theravada Buddhist scriptures and chants (if not Pali, the language of the word is noted). They are brief translations for quick reference: these are not exhaustive or refined definitions. Not all of the foreign words found in the talks are listed below, as many are defined at the point of use. Note: most Pali diacritics have been omitted here and within the book, as few people are familiar with the specialized pronunciation conventions.

ajahn *(Thai)* 'teacher'. Often used as the title of the senior monk or monks at a monastery.

anagarika 'homeless one'. An anagarika, still technically a lay person, lives in a monastery and follows the Eight Precepts.

anatta 'not-self', i.e. impersonal, without individual essence.

anicca impermanent, transient (and by implication, ephemeral), having the nature to arise and pass away.

arahant an enlightened being, free from all delusion.

bhavana practice, cultivation. Used in a specific way (e.g., *metta bhavana*), or more generally (as in the *bhavana* which the spiritual life itself entails).

bhikkhu alms mendicant. In Buddhism, it is the term for a monk, who lives on alms and abides by training precepts which define a life of renunciation and simplicity.

bodhisatta As used in the Theravada school, this refers to a being destined for enlightenment, and sometimes specifically to Gotama Buddha before his enlightenment.

bodhisattva *(Sanskrit)* A term from Mahayana Buddhism, referring to one who 'delays complete enlightenment' for the sake of helping other beings reach enlightenment first.

Buddha The Understanding One, the One who is awake, who knows things as they are; a potential in every human being. The historical Buddha, Siddhattha Gotama, lived and taught between 563 and 483 BC.

Chao Khun *(Thai)* title of honour for a monk, which confers responsibility for the Sangha of a district.

dana generosity. Hence, often used to refer to an offering, especially of food, to a monastic community.

dhamma This word is used in several ways. It can refer to the Buddha's Teaching, as contained in the scriptures; to the Ultimate Truth, towards which the teaching points; and to a discrete 'moment' of life, seen as it really is. (Sanskrit: 'dharma'.)

dhutanga (*Thai:* **tudong**) special strict monastic observances. *Dhutanga bhikkhus* are noted for their diligence and impeccability. In Thailand, such monks often undertake the mendicant's wandering practice of the Buddha's time – hence the phrase, 'to wander (or 'go') *tudong*'.

dukkha 'hard to bear'; dis-ease, restlessness of mind, discontent or suffering, anguish, conflict, unsatisfactoriness.

jhana meditative absorption or trance.

kamma action or cause (and by extension, the result or effect) which is created or recreated by habitual impulse, volitions, natural energies. (Sanskrit: 'karma'.)

karuna compassion.

khandha 'heap'; the term the Buddha used to refer to each of the five components of human psycho-physical existence.

koan *(Japanese)* meditation riddle, often used in the Zen form of Buddhism.

kuti *(Thai)* hut; typical abode of a forest monastery *bhikkhu*.

Luang Por *(Thai)* difficult to translate; literally, 'Venerable Father', but very much conveying a sense of affection as well as respect.

Mara a being of Buddhist mythology who is the adversary of the Buddha; hence, the one who tempts, deludes or destroys. *Mara* is also the Pali word for 'death'.

metta goodwill, 'loving-kindness'.

mudita 'sympathetic' joy (the opposite of jealousy).

Nibbana freedom from attachments. The basis for the enlightened vision of things as they are. (Sanskrit: 'Nirvana'.)

pañña discriminative wisdom.

paramita (*Thai:* **parami**) 'Perfections' or 'superlative virtues', qualities especially recommended by the Buddha for those seeking enlightenment.

Phra Khru *(Thai)* title of honour for a monk, recognizing his service as a teacher.

Precepts (Five/Eight/Ten) The basic codes of conduct recommended by the Buddha for his followers. The Five Precepts pertain to the ordinary 'household' life, and the Eight or Ten Precepts form the foundation for the renunciant life (which is then further elaborated in the *vinaya*). A list of the Precepts is given at the end of this glossary.

samadhi concentration or one-pointedness of mind.

samana one who has entered the Holy Life; a religious.

samanera (*Thai:* **samanen**) The novice stage for a bhikkhu. A samanera lives within the Ten Precepts, but does not yet follow the complete *bhikkhu-vinaya*.

samsara the unenlightened, unsatisfactory experience of life.

sila moral virtue.

sangha the community of those who practise the Buddha's Way. Often, more specifically, those who have formally committed themselves to the lifestyle of a mendicant monk or nun.

sati mindfulness, recollection.

sukha happiness.

sutta a Buddhist scripture.

tudong *see 'dhutanga' above.*

upajjhaya 'preceptor', a bhikkhu who may admit others into the monastic order.

upasampada ceremony of entering the *bhikkhu-sangha*; bhikkhu 'ordination'.

upekkha equanimity, serenity.

uposatha the Buddhist 'Sabbath', a day which lay people often spend at a monastery, observing the Eight Precepts. The *uposatha* days occur according to the lunar phases.

vassa the 'Rains' retreat period. As established by the Buddha, it occurs during the Asian monsoon season.

vihara a residence; often used as the name for a small monastery.

vinaya the monastic discipline, or the scriptural collection of its rules and commentaries.

vipassana the penetrative insight of meditation, as distinguished from simple mental tranquillity.

wat pah *(Thai)* forest monastery (typically, a place of *dhutanga* observance).

THE PRECEPTS

The Five, Eight or Ten Precepts are guidelines which encourage mindfulness and selfless action. They are best understood as the proper standards of behaviour for a human being, to be respected and cultivated. Shortcomings with regard to the precepts do not necessarily constitute sin or evil, but rather they point out where greater effort and awareness are needed. The practice of the precepts is beneficial both to the one who uses them and to those who encounter such a person.

The first five are recommended for all people:

1 Not intentionally taking the life of any living creature.

2 Not taking anything which is not given.

3 Refraining from irresponsible sexual conduct.
(As part of the Eight or Ten Precepts, this is observed as complete chastity, i.e. refraining from any sexual behaviour.)

4 Not speaking falsely, abusively or maliciously.

5 Not taking any intoxicating drink or drug.

The next three are the traditional renunciations helpful to those engaged in serious spiritual practice:

6 Not taking solid food after mid-day.

7 Not singing, playing music, dancing, or attending games and shows; not beautifying or adorning one's body.

8 Not using a high or luxurious sleeping place.

To arrive at ten precepts (which form the basis of mendicancy), one divides the seventh into two precepts, and then adds the following:

10 Not handling or controlling money.